THE
NARWHAL

THE
NARWHAL
UNICORN OF THE SEA

FRED BRUEMMER

KEY PORTER BOOKS

With love for Heddy, Hella and Arist

Canadian Cataloguing in Publication Data
Bruemmer, Fred
  The narwhal: unicorn of the sea

ISBN 1-55013-187-7

1. Narwhal—Pictorial works. 2. Unicorns—Pictorial works. I. Title.

QL737.C433B7 1993   599.5'3   C90-095357-8

Key Porter Books Limited
70 The Esplanade
Toronto, Ontario
Canada M5E 1R2

Distributed in the United States of America by:
Publishers Group West
4065 Hollis
Emeryville, CA   94608

Typesetting: Compeer Typographic Services Limited
Printed on acid-free paper
Printed and bound in Hong Kong

93 94 95 96 97 6 5 4 3 2 1

Page 1: *A painting of a tusked male narwhal and its tuskless mate by Richard Ellis.*
Page 2: *A pod of ivory-tusked narwhals.* Janet Foster/Masterfile

CONTENTS

PREFACE

I have spent half a lifetime in the Arctic, often in pursuit of narwhals. I am deeply grateful to Dr. Arthur W. Mansfield of the Arctic Biological Station, Department of Fisheries and Oceans, for his permission to join his narwhal study team at Koluktoo Bay in 1965 and for his subsequent help and friendship. Brian Beck, who headed that team and is now with the Bedford Institute of Oceanography, has remained a good and generous friend despite my atrocious cooking.

I returned to Koluktoo Bay in 1988 with two outstanding scientists, Dr. Michael Kingsley of Canada's Department of Fisheries and Oceans and Dr. Malcolm Ramsay of the University of Saskatchewan. I thank them both for letting me join their narwhal study and for sharing their knowledge of the North with me. Holly Cleator of Winnipeg's Freshwater Institute shared her narwhal observations with me and for that I am most grateful. I very much appreciated the long conversations with Sheatie Tagak of Pond Inlet, Baffin Island; they helped me to understand the present-day narwhal hunter's point of view.

The Polar Inuit of northwest Greenland, with whom I lived for more than half a year, taught me what narwhal hunting meant and means to the natives of the North.

Dr. Thomas G. Smith, Dr. Edward Mitchell, Wyb Hoek and Gary Sleno of the Department of Fisheries and Oceans have helped me with my narwhal research over many years; their friendship and kindness is greatly appreciated. To Randall Reeves I am grateful for sharing with me his phenomenal knowledge of whales and the history of whaling.

Canada's Polar Continental Shelf Project has assisted my arctic research and for this I am grateful, especially to George Hobson, its former director, and to its base managers Barry L. Hough, Eddie Chapman and Jim Godden.

Dr. J.E. Lewis of Atlantic Marine Wildlife Tours Ltd. made it possible for me to spend time at the floe edge near Pond Inlet. Jim Allan of Ecosummer Expeditions enabled me to visit Skraeling Island in the highest Arctic. I am grateful to both of them.

Richard Ellis is one of the world's foremost painters of marine life. I am very grateful for his permission to use his superb narwhal paintings in this book.

Editor Laurie Coulter tracked down and obtained the unicorn pictures. I thank her for her patience and perseverance and for always being so very nice and so superbly organized.

Above all, I thank my wife, Maud, for sharing my life, my dreams and my search for the unicorn.

The summer realm of the narwhal: Radstock Bay, Devon Island, off Lancaster Sound.

THE BAY OF WHALES

In the Schatzkammer, the Imperial Treasury, in Vienna, the splendor and
wealth of the Habsburg empire is on display: the 1,000-year-old crown of the
Holy Roman Empire, first used in the year 962 for the coronation of Otto the
Great in Rome, made of pure gold and covered with great rubies, pearls and
emeralds; the Holy Lance that supposedly pierced the body of Christ on the
Cross; the sumptuous coronation robes of the emperors.

Among these great treasures are four made of *ainkhürn*, a quaint and ancient
dialect word for *Einhorn*, the unicorn. The shaft of the crosier once carried by
the bishops of Vienna is the horn of a unicorn. The scabbard and hilt of the
Ainkhürn Schwert, the unicorn sword, are covered with plates of unicorn horn,
the polished ivory yellow with age. It once belonged to Charles the Bold
(1433–77), last reigning duke of Burgundy. The very scepter of the Habsburgs,
symbol of their imperial power and authority, created for the Emperor Matthias
in 1612 by one of the greatest craftsmen of the age, Andreas Osenbruck of
Prague, is made of *ainkhürn* beset with large diamonds, rubies, sapphires and
emeralds. Standing alone on a dark wooden base, secured by metal clamps, is a
single, spiraled horn, two-and-a-half inches thick at the base and slightly more
than six feet tall, marked simply *Das Ainkhürn*. It, too, had once belonged to
the house of Burgundy and was part of the dowry Mary of Burgundy brought to
Vienna when she married Emperor Maximilian I in 1477. As I looked at it in
the spring of 1989, a French family passed by and a little boy asked, "Qu'est-ce
que c'est, Papa?" and without a second's hesitation the father replied, "C'est
la corne de la licorne"—"That is the horn of the unicorn."

It is, in fact, the tusk of the narwhal, the small whale of the High Arctic
which the American author and explorer Ivan T. Sanderson has called ". . .
the most extraordinary of all living mammals." All the *ainkhürns* in the Habsburg collection are narwhal tusks, as are nearly all "unicorn horns" in the
treasuries, palaces and museums of the world: the "Horn of Windsor," which
Queen Elizabeth I valued at £10,000, a sum which in 16th-century Britain
would buy an estate complete with castle; the three "unicorn horns" of the
doges, now in the treasury of St. Mark's Basilica in Venice; the horns that
make up the "unicorn throne" of the Danish kings; and the crossed unicorn
horns in the entrance hall of the Korinkaku Palace of Prince Takamatsu in

Japan. The narwhal of the remote arctic seas was the principal, though anonymous, parent of the unicorn. But while the unicorn has been famous for at least 4,000 years, the ivory-tusked narwhal swam far beyond most of mankind's ken. Noted the American author-naturalist Barry Lopez in 1986, "We know more about the rings of Saturn than we know about the narwhal."

The unicorn, magnificent and mysterious, has pervaded human thought and art as has perhaps no other animal, real or imagined. Albrecht Dürer painted it and so did Leonardo da Vinci. Raphael painted a beautiful lady holding a little unicorn in her arms. The Florentine sculptor and goldsmith Benvenuto Cellini cast it in gold, and the most glorious tapestries ever woven are the seven *Unicorn Tapestries* that once belonged to the Counts de la Rochefoucauld and now hang in The Cloisters in New York. Powerful and pure, the unicorn was a medieval ideograph for Christ. Albertus Magnus, the famous 13th-century scholar-priest, wrote, "This unicorn is Christ whose might, typified by its horn, is irresistible."

Its magic horn was said to cure all ills from ague to plague. The great unicorn horn of Saint-Denis near Paris (a seven-foot-long narwhal tusk that weighed 13 pounds) stood in a marble basin filled with water. All the sick who flocked to the famous monastery drank the water believing that it would heal them. It was mankind's firm belief, held for thousands of years, that unicorn horn could also detect and neutralize poison. These horns were thus among the most prized possessions of poison-prone princes and potentates. The eating utensils of the kings of France were made of unicorn horn until the revolution made such precautions superfluous, and other monarchs spent fortunes to acquire the precious horns. A German prince, the margrave of Bayreuth, paid "six hundred thousand rix-dollars" for his unicorn horn.

The griffin and the basilisk, manticore and mermecolion, chimaera, dragon, phoenix and peryton — the entire weird and wonderful menagerie that once roamed through the medieval mind — are wholly forgotten or barely remembered. All vanished except the unicorn whose magic beguiles us still. Aloof and magnificent, pure and eternal, it is an embodiment of man's desires and aspirations. Of it the German poet Rainer Maria Rilke wrote:

O here's the beast that no existence hath.
By sight they knew it not yet held it dear.

. . . .
And from its brow there sprouted out a horn
One unique horn.

The narwhal, too, has fascinated poets. Pablo Neruda, the Nobel-prize winning Chilean poet and diplomat, once owned a narwhal tusk and extolled the mystic beauty of the narwhal and the unicorn: "The land unicorn lives on

The elegant Ainkhürn Schwert, the unicorn sword in Vienna, covered with plates of narwhal ivory, once belonged to Duke Charles the Bold. Kunsthistorisches Museum, Vienna

Leonardo da Vinci's sketch of a lady with a unicorn. He also wrote a treatise on how to capture unicorns. Ashmolean Museum, Oxford

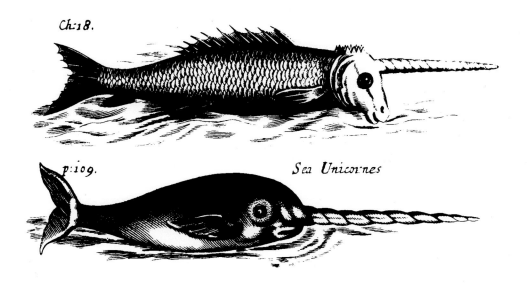

Pierre Pomet published his Histoire des Drogues *in Paris in 1694. In the English edition the "sea unicorn" is shown above and the "narwhal" below. Both carry the identical spiraled narwhal tusk.* Metropolitan Toronto Library Board

forever in tapestries, a dazzling creature surrounded by alabastrine ladies with high coiffures, aureoled in its majesty by birds that trill or flash their brilliant plumage. As for the narwhal, medieval monarchs considered it a magnificent gift and sent one another fragments of its fabulous horn. From it one scraped a powder which, diluted in liqueurs, bestowed — O eternal dream of man! — health, youth, and virility!" But, he mused, "Does the narwhal exist? Can such an extraordinary sea creature with an ivory lance four or five meters long on his brow . . . can it and its legend, its marvelous name, go unnoticed by millions of human beings?" He concluded, "The sea unicorn is shrouded in mystery . . . with its long ivory sword submerged in unexplored oceans."

The fact that the narwhal lived in the most inaccessible seas of the Arctic enabled the narwhal-unicorn connection to become one of the best-kept trade secrets of all time. The Inuit and the tribes that inhabited Siberia's northern coasts knew the narwhal, but they, like the narwhal, were isolated from the rest of the world. The Vikings hunted the narwhal and also obtained tusks in trade from arctic natives. They sold these tusks as unicorn horns and said as little as possible about their true origin. The middlemen who carried the tusks to Europe and the Middle East, to China and Japan, seldom knew that these horns were the enormously elongated teeth of an arctic whale and, if they did, kept the knowledge to themselves. It was, after all, in everyone's interest to maintain the unicorn legend. At the peak of its prestige and popularity, unicorn horn was worth ten times its weight in gold, and for large horns rulers paid what in today's terms would be millions of dollars. And, finally, to the vast majority of people, the existence of a horselike animal carrying a wonder-working horn, vouched for by Aristotle, Pliny and the Bible, seemed infinitely more believable than the existence of a whale with a ten-foot-long ivory tusk. (In the early 1960s a mechanic, newly arrived in an arctic settlement, saw some

Inuit haul a great male narwhal ashore. He walked over, looked at the tusked whale in wonder, and finally said, "There ain't no such animal!")

This veil of secrecy was slightly lifted by the first arctic explorers who reported seeing "sea-unicorns" or found their horns upon arctic shores. The existence of a second unicorn, this one of the sea, created great confusion. The English explorer Richard Chancellor, searching for the Northeast Passage in 1553, was greatly heartened when he found a narwhal tusk upon the shore of Russia's White Sea. "Knowing that Unycorns are bredde in the landes of Cathaye," he felt certain that China was near. His contemporary and rival, Sir Humphrey Gilbert, a passionate proponent of the Northwest Passage, refuted and ridiculed Chancellor's claim. The horn, he said, could not have drifted from China to the White Sea "being of such a nature that it will not swimme," and furthermore "there is a fish which hath but one horne in his forehead like to an Unicorne, and therefore it seemeth very doubtfull both from whence it came, and whether it was an Unicornes horne, yea, or nay."

Only in the 19th century did explorers, closely followed by whalers, breach the Middle Pack. This mighty ice barrier in northern Davis Strait, between Baffin Island and Greenland, shielded Baffin Bay and the adjacent sounds, straits and inlets, sanctuary to most of the world's narwhals. With the end of the Napoleonic Wars, the British navy had ships and men to spare and, prodded by Sir Joseph Banks, president of the prestigious Royal Society, it resumed the quest for the Northwest Passage, the Holy Grail of arctic exploration. In the spring of 1818 two ships commanded by Captain John Ross and Lieutenant William Edward Parry sailed for Greenland. Among the gifts they carried for any Far North natives they might encounter were 15 pounds of vermilion paint, 102 pounds of snuff, 13 cases of beads and cowrie shells, and 40 umbrellas. Ross rammed his ships through the Middle Pack and emerged into the North Water, the largest polynya in the Arctic, a sea area that due to strong currents and upwelling water never freezes. This sea was full of life. John Ross saw "myriad . . . of the little awk [dovekie], swimming on the water, together with vast numbers of whales [bowhead whales] and sea unicorns . . . These whales are not only numerous, but, from their never having been disturbed, tame, and easily approached."

On August 8, 1818, in northern Melville Bay, Ross saw men on the ice. The Polar Inuit had been discovered, a people, then numbering only about 200, so totally isolated for many centuries "that we found them ignorant . . . that there were other people in the world than themselves, or other places than the spot they occupied." Their main food was seal and narwhal meat and fat, and since they lacked wood, narwhal tusks were vitally important to them. Ross gave them presents and in return received "a spear made of sea-unicorn's horn . . . and a sledge, made chiefly of the bones of the seal, tied together with thong of seal-skin; the runners . . . being formed of sea-unicorn's horns." Ross sailed on

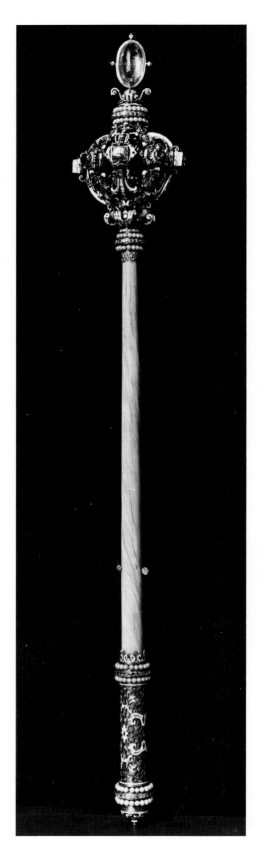

The magnificent scepter of the Habsburgs was made of a narwhal's tusk. Kunsthistorisches Museum, Vienna

Because it was firmly believed that unicorn horn could detect and neutralize poison, drinking vessels of poison-prone princes were made of it. Kunsthistorisches Museum, Vienna

to search for the Northwest Passage, but when he found it, he was tricked by one of those mirages so common in the Arctic; he thought the entrance to Lancaster Sound was barred by mountains and returned to London.

Parry, who had not seen the mirage mountains, returned the following year, battled heavy ice and suddenly emerged into the relatively ice-free Lancaster Sound. He was amazed and delighted; he had discovered an arctic Eden, "the headquarters of the whales." Giant bowhead whales lolled lazily in the dark sea. On July 30, Parry and his crew counted 89. "Sea-horses" (walruses) lay "huddled together like pigs" and were "stupidly tame." Polar bears ambled nonchalantly across the ice floes. White whales "were swimming about the ships in great numbers" with "a shrill, ringing sound, not unlike that of musical glasses badly played." Sleek narwhals, "called sea-unicorns by the sailors," surged through the sea. Eden, however, was quickly defiled. On August 11, the sailors "succeeded in harpooning a narwhal" and, Parry noted proudly, "thus has a new and extensive field been opened for one of the most lucrative branches of our commerce."

For the whalers the bowhead was the ideal whale. Slow, timid and very fat, it had a ton or more of baleen in its mouth, worth at one time $6 a pound. In the days before plastics, baleen—a tough, resilient, keratinous substance—had many uses. Shredded and colored, it was made into the panache on knights' helmets, or used to stuff chairs and bolsters. Ramrods were made of it, as were fishing rods, umbrella ribs and the springs of the first typewriters. Most important, "whalebone" was needed for women's stays and corsets, and the hoops of their voluminous skirts. The poet Alexander Pope (1688–1744) said of the ladies of his day, they were "stiff with hoops, and arm'd with ribs of whale." So valuable was baleen, that at one time a single bowhead whale could pay for a two-year whaling voyage. A hundred years after Parry discovered their High Arctic summer haunts, the great whales had been hunted to the edge of extinction. Today, after 70 years of protection, only about 300 bowheads survive in the entire eastern Arctic, a sea area many times the size of France.

The narwhal was smaller, faster, more elusive and less valuable than the bowhead whale. To whalers it was incidental prey but an augury of bowheads. In early summer when harp seals, bowheads and narwhals swam northward, part of a complex annual migration that has only recently been understood and mapped, they often passed explorers and whalers. Robert Peary on his way to the North Pole admired "a school of narwhal dashing to windward, their long white horns flashing out of the water in regular cadence, the waves dashing jets of spray from their bluff foreheads."

On July 1, 1866, Charles Edward Smith, doctor aboard the British whaler *Diana*, wrote in his diary: "Many thousands of narwhales have been passing the ship today, all heading up the Sound [Lancaster Sound] in little companies. The captain tells me they always make their appearance here at this time, and

An inukshuk, *an ancient man-shaped Inuit marker, stands upon a cliff overlooking Hudson Strait.*

are sure indicators of the presence of whales [bowheads], the whales appearing immediately after the narwhales." The whalers, who called narwhals "unies" or "unicorns," had a saying: "After seals unies, and after unicorns whales." People of 19th-century Europe and America regarded sea mammal hunting as lucrative, heroic and romantic, the way wars were once regarded. Henry Wadsworth Longfellow caught that spirit to perfection in a poem about the Arctic:

There we hunted the walrus, the narwhal and the seal.
Aha! 'twas a noble game:
And like the lightning's flame,
Flew our harpoons of steel.

Most narwhals are bound for Lancaster Sound. In late June or early July, 15,000 migrate into it in just a few days. Another 2,000 cluster near the ice-choked entrance to Pond Inlet, which separates Bylot and Baffin islands. They wait anxiously for the ice to break so they can seek summer refuge in a remote bay more than 100 miles inland, which the Inuit call Koluktoo, "the bay of waterfalls." But before the narwhals can reach that bay, they must run a deadly gauntlet of Inuit hunters and killer whales.

In late June, wrote the explorer-author Peter Freuchen, who was in the Pond Inlet region in 1924, the Inuit gathered at Button Point on Bylot Island "awaiting the great event of their year—the day the narwhal comes toward land." At the same time "every year a school of killer whales shows up . . . and the narwhals come fleeing into the leads." Beyond the edge of the ice, killer whales with high dorsal fins, loath to enter the ice, "travel up and down to keep watch." The fleeing narwhals, swimming in narrow leads of open water, were easy prey for the Inuit hunters. "And thus," said Freuchen, "several hundred narwhals are usually killed by the natives every year."

In open water, the powerful killer whales hunt the hapless narwhals with relentless speed and military precision. The scientist Hermann Steltner, a long-time resident of the village of Pond Inlet, watched such an attack while in a boat on Eclipse Sound on August 30, 1980. At 3:45 p.m., he and his wife saw several herds of narwhals "in full flight and . . . a large herd of Killer Whales moving . . . at an even greater speed . . . their bellies and eye patches flashing white." The hunting pack consisted of 30 to 40 large killer whales and "whale screams could be heard . . . as the Killer Whale herd passed right through the Narwhal herds." The hunters split into several groups, and by 5:05 p.m., the "Narwhals [about 200] were completely encircled by the killers . . . Suddenly all breathing noise ceased and everything was quiet." At 5:14 p.m., "the Killer Whales started to attack . . . the waters were whipped white by thrashing whales. At one point a Narwhal was seen rolling sideways on the surface, its mouth open in high-pitched screams."

The fleeing narwhals follow the receding ice through Eclipse Sound, past the brooding cliffs that face Milne Inlet and emerge, usually in early August, in Koluktoo Bay, where meltwater in lacy, wind-ripped waterfalls pours down dark mountain sides. There, in 1965, I spent six grueling weeks with Brian Beck and David Robb, technicians at Canada's Arctic Biological Station. Fighting ice and vicious storms, we set nets, captured narwhals, dissected them, collected data, and cached mounds of meat and fat for the Inuit of Pond Inlet. The study had been initiated by Dr. Arthur Mansfield, one of Canada's foremost sea mammal specialists, to gain some understanding of this little known whale.

All around us at Koluktoo Bay were signs of long-ago hunters: house ruins, now lush with plants, of Thule culture Inuit who used bowhead bones to build their dwellings; broken tools, many made of narwhal tusk; large whale bones on the beach, gray with age, and, in their lee, clusters of plants deriving shelter and nutrients from the decaying bones. The very stones that held our tents had been used for hundreds, perhaps thousands, of years to hold the sealskin tents of Inuit narwhal hunters upon this same storm-lashed beach. Our tents were held up with aluminum poles, theirs with poles made of narwhal tusks. We set our giant nets, a deadly wall of 18-inch nylon mesh into the green pellucid water, then spent frantic days and nights racing our canoes through storms and waves to save the nets from being shredded by wind-driven ice fields.

On August 19, a rare calm day, the narwhals came into Koluktoo Bay. Suddenly the air was filled with the explosive "pooff," "pooff," "pooff" of breathing whales, with their high-pitched squeals, like balloons rubbed together, their groans and grunts, and once with a deep, melancholy tuba note, drawn out and infinitely sad. Most whales, in groups of five to twenty, swam far out in the bay. A few strayed close to shore that day and died in our nets.

We captured 17 narwhals, a welcome windfall for the Inuit of the region, who came in boats to collect them. (When I returned to Koluktoo Bay 23 years later, an Inuk in his forties smiled and said, "Oh yes, I remember when you were here. That was the year we had lots to eat!") It was nearly always stormy, and we were dirty, wet and tired. Just before we left, the weather changed and there came one of those rare days when the Arctic is sublime — the snowfields golden, the sky a tracery of purple clouds. Great peace filled land and sea. We heard the resounding "swoosh" of a surfacing narwhal. A great male headed straight for the net nearest to our camp. David and I ran over. The bay was calm for once, somber bronze in the afterglow of the setting sun. As we stood on the cliff above the net, the narwhal hit it and began its silent, desperate struggle for life, deep down in the dark water. The great styrofoam floats bobbed up and down in a macabre jig of death, spreading concentric circles across the surface of the placid sea. After 15 minutes, a stream of glistening bubbles pearled towards the surface, rested there an instant, popped and vanished. The sea unicorn was dead, and we returned to camp silent and thoughtful.

This beautifully carved narwhal tusk is in London's Victoria and Albert Museum. By courtesy of the Board of Trustees of the Victoria and Albert Museum

The harsh coast of Bylot Island in spring. In June the ice cracks, leads open and narwhals swim towards Koluktoo Bay where they will spend the summer.

DAWN IN CHINA

Huang-ti, the legendary Yellow Emperor of China, is said to have reigned for a hundred years, from 2697 BC to 2597 BC. He united China, built its first great palace and compiled a calendar. His wife, the Empress Si Ling-chi, invented sericulture, the raising of silkworms to produce the famous silk of China. As befitted such a beneficial reign, it was ushered in by the first recorded appearance of a unicorn. Chinese chroniclers say that in 2697 BC, the year of the emperor's birth, a *k'i-lin*, a "great unicorn," walked majestically into the imperial manor, roamed its halls and vanished.

The Chinese unicorn had a stag's body, the hoofs of a horse and the tail of an ox. Unlike the unicorn of the West, often depicted as pure white, the Chinese unicorn had a coat of five colors. From its flame-colored brow sprouted a 12-foot-long horn. It was immensely powerful, but quiet, wise and noble. The Argentinian poet Jorge Luis Borges has noted that the Chinese unicorn "is so gentle that when it walks it is careful not to tread on the tiniest living creature and will not even eat live grass but only what is dead."

Of China's four animals of good omen — unicorn, dragon, phoenix and tortoise — the unicorn was the most auspicious. Its sudden appearance foretold the birth of a great and just ruler or of a person of great worth. (Hopeful Chinese brides traditionally carried images of unicorns.) In the 6th century BC, according to legend, a young woman, Yen Chen-tsai, was walking in her garden when a unicorn suddenly entered. It knelt before her and gave her the jade tablet it carried in its mouth. Upon it was written:

Son of mountain crystal
When the dynasty crumbles,
thou shalt rule as a throneless king.

Shortly afterwards her son was born. He was Confucius, China's greatest sage, its "throneless king."

Unicorn horn was called *ku-tu-si* (or *tu-na-si*). Most horns were the tusks of narwhals and, as in the West, it was widely believed that they could cure most illnesses and detect and neutralize poison. The 4th-century author Li Shih-chen advised that "the [unicorn] horn is a safe guide to tell the presence of

Above: *Now in a St. Petersburg museum, the famous Berezovka mammoth was found nearly intact in 1900 in Siberia.*

Opposite: *Samarkand, the ancient city of Central Asia, was a center of the silk and ivory trade from China to the Middle East and of the ivory trade from the Arctic to the Arab lands. It also was the sumptuous capital of Tamerlane, who is buried beneath the majestic dome of the Gur Emir.*

poison: when poisonous medicines of liquid form are stirred with a horn, a white foam will bubble up, and no other test is necessary.''

Unicorn horn was not the only substance in China that could defeat poison; healers also used the twisted body of an ancient snake. This, too, according to the famous orientalist Berthold Laufer, was really a narwhal tusk: "The 'thousand-years-old snake' [of the Chinese pharmacopoeia] is nothing but the fossil narwhal [tusk] occurring on the northern shores of Siberia, especially in the valley of the Kolyma River."

From China the unicorn and its legends (and perhaps some of its horns) traveled to Japan. The German art historian A. Brockhaus noted in his monograph on *netsuke*, the beautifully carved kimono toggles, that many were made of narwhal ivory. The narwhal tusk, he wrote, "was taken during the Middle Ages in Japan for the horn of the unicorn, being regarded as an infallible antidote against poison and paid dearer than gold."

One western traveler who actually saw an Asian "unicorn" was the Venetian Marco Polo (1254–1324). On the island of Sumatra (now part of Indonesia), he reported "there are many wild elephants and unicorns, the latter much smaller than the elephant but with similar feet . . . In the middle of the forehead they have a single horn. Their head is like that of a wild boar and they carry it low, towards the ground. They take delight in muddy pools and are filthy in their habits. They are not at all like those [unicorns] which are said to allow themselves to be taken by maidens, but are of a quite contrary nature."

The unicorn Marco Polo describes quite accurately is the now rare (about 500 are left) one-horned Sumatran rhinoceros. It is headed for extinction, as are all other rhinoceros species, because its horn is still valued by the Chinese as a panacea, by the Japanese as an aphrodisiac, and by the Yemenis as handles for their *jambiyyas*, the beautiful carved daggers most men wear. In Macao, the tiny Portuguese colony on the South China coast, rhino horn was sold in pharmacies in 1981 for $450 an ounce. In Mandalay, Burma, rhinoceros horn cost $20,000 a kilogram in 1984. Even rhino urine is valuable. Some Asian zoos collect and sell it: it is drunk in the belief that it will cure sore throats and ward off asthma attacks. Unicorn and rhinoceros myths often merged; the wonder-working qualities of one were ascribed to the other. Today's dying rhinos are the victims of an ancient legend.

Unicorn lore is aswirl with confusion because the unicorn was really a composite, a beast with several parents. One was the oryx, the horselike antelope of Africa and parts of Asia. It was often represented in silhouette, which made it appear as if it had only a single annulated (but not spiraled) horn. In 1656 the Carmelite friar Vincenzo Maria saw oryxes in Muscat: "large as stags, similar to them in shape but . . . they are the purest white . . . I myself believe these creatures to be those which some writers describe as the Unicorn, some of which were found in the olden days in Mecca . . ."

". . . Unycorns are bredde in the landes of Cathaye."

— RICHARD CHANCELLOR, English arctic explorer, 1553

A *Spitsbergen whaling scene published in London in 1705. Crews kill and haul back bowhead whales, a "sea-unicorn" lies in the shallows and a walrus is on the beach.* National Archives of Canada/C 27579

The hapless rhinoceros was another parent. Its horn was believed to have the same antidotal properties as unicorn horn, and from remotest antiquity rhino horns, beautifully bound with golden bands, were used as poison-proof drinking cups by Indian princes and Chinese nobles. Aelian, the Roman author of *De Animalium Natura*, a 2nd-century collection of animal tales, wrote that in India kings drank from vessels of "unicorn horn" and "they decorate the horn with golden rings at intervals." If poisoned liquid was poured into such a goblet, the horn, it was said, began to sweat and change color. A few of these "assay cups," as they were called, found their way to the West. The Holy Roman Emperor Rudolf II (1552–1612) owned a "unicorn cup" of rhinoceros horn. It is now in the National Museum in Copenhagen.

And, finally, there was the undeniable existence of the arctic narwhal's spiraled tusk, which, although its true origin was a carefully guarded secret, was thought by all to be the horn of the *unicornum verum*, "the real unicorn."

The Chinese, of course, knew the rhinoceros and valued its horn but not

*Great glaciers flow into Alexandra Fiord,
Ellesmere Island, where, long ago, Thule
Culture Inuit hunted narwhals.*

Sculpted by wind and waves, icebergs drift
past the Baffin Island coast.

A white whale rolls and splashes in the
shallows, probably to scratch itchy, molting
skin on the rocks.

nearly as much as *ku-tu-si*, the infinitely more precious horn of the much rarer unicorn. When the Emperor Marcus Aurelius sent the first Roman embassy to China in 166, it stopped in southern India and bought there, as gifts for China, elephant tusks, rhinoceros horns and tortoise shells, things that were immensely valuable in Rome. In China, where the most valuable ivory came from the north, these gifts were considered cheap and commonplace and, as a result, the Roman embassy was poorly received.

The narwhal-unicorn connection was further muddled because the trade routes of narwhal tusks were identical with those that brought walrus tusks and mammoth ivory to China and the Middle East. Narwhals were once common in the arctic seas north of Siberia and European Russia. In 1895, the Norwegian explorer Fridtjof Nansen, sledging towards the North Pole, came to badly broken ice at 83°N and "found the lanes about here full of narwhals." Walruses were hunted by arctic natives from Russia's White Sea to Siberia's Kamchatka Peninsula. And mammoth bones and tusks were so common in Siberia that Catherine the Great of Russia (1729–1796) in her correspondence with Voltaire several times expressed the hope that a live mammoth would be found. She sent out an expedition, but after nine years of searching, Martin Sauer reported that "Mammout's tusks are found about the Siberian rivers and the shores of the Icy Sea, and scattered all over the arctic flats." But, he concluded regretfully, "It appears that the animal is extinct."

The greatest concentration of mammoth tusks was on the bleak New Siberian Islands. There, in 1809, the Swedish explorer Hedenström "in the space of a verst [about half a mile]" saw "ten tusks of elephants [mammoths] sticking up in the sand and gravel . . . and a large sandbank was always covered with tusks after a gale." On the same islands the Russian surveyor Chvoinoff had found in 1775 masses of mammoth tusks and many "long . . . screw-formed bones," the tusks of narwhals. Hedenström, too, had seen "three narwhals . . . enclosed in the ice . . . at the mouth of the Yana" river in Siberia.

The Chinese called the mammoth *yin shu*, "the giant mole," and believed it to be a subterranean rodent that perished when it came to the surface. As in so many legends, there was some truth in this. Entire mammoths, preserved by ice, were found from time to time in Siberia; they protruded from the permafrost and were invariably dead. From at least the 4th century BC, China obtained more than half of its ivory from the imperishable tusks of the mammoth—about 7,000 tons, the ivory of 50,000 mammoths, in the past 350 years alone. (There is plenty left. Antony J. Sutcliffe, curator of Pleistocene mammals at the British Museum, wrote in 1985 that an estimated 550,000 tons of mammoth ivory still lie buried along the 600-mile coast between the rivers Yana and Kolyma. This is also the area where in former days most narwhal tusks were found.)

The North, then, had three types of ivory—walrus, mammoth and narwhal

"The ultimate destination of the [narwhal] ivory is China, where it is used . . . for medicine, and for the manufacture of cups, supposed to absorb all poisons placed in them."

— A.P. Low, Canadian geologist and explorer, 1903

—worth fortunes in the wealthy South. The ivory reached the lucrative markets of China and the Middle East by four main trade routes used since antiquity.

The first trade route led from Baghdad to Samarkand in Central Asia, the city Alexander the Great knew as Maracanda, and on to the ancient city of Novgorod on Lake Ilmen (southeast of today's St. Petersburg). Several Russian towns held annual fur fairs; the most famous one was in Novgorod. The furs—lustrous sable, silky vair and the pelts of polar bears — and the arctic ivory offered for sale at the fair usually reached the Middle East by such intermediaries as the Bulgars (or Bolgars), a Turkic people living on the lower Volga (the name "Volga" is derived from "Bolgar"). But some enterprising traders came all the way from Baghdad to the fair at Novgorod by camel and dog team. The Arab merchant-diplomat Ibn-Fadlan visited Novgorod in the winter of 922 and reported to his master, the caliph of Baghdad, that the natives of the Far North had come to the fair, with furs and ivory, "on boards eight or nine ells long"—skis!

On the second route, described by the 14th-century Arab writer-explorer Ibn Batuta, merchants traveled from Persia across the Caspian Sea to the Bolgars of the lower Volga and then "in small cars drawn by dogs" for 40 days to the "Land of Darkness" north of the Arctic Circle (probably the Perm or Pechora regions west of the Urals). In exchange for furs and ivory, they gave the arctic people steel blades "to cast into the Dark Sea" to harpoon narwhals and walruses. It was probably by this route that Tsar Boris Godunov (1551–1605) sent a delegation to Persia to negotiate an alliance against the Turks. His gift to Shah Abbas the Great was seven *rogozubi*, the Old Russian name for narwhal tusks. In return for the seven narwhal tusks, the shah gave the tsar a magnificent gold-covered throne, glittering with 2,200 precious stones and pearls, which one can still admire in the Kremlin "Armory," the fabulous treasury of the tsars.

The third route, much farther east, funneled walrus, narwhal and mammoth ivory from Siberia to Khiva, an ancient city on the Amu-Darya River in Central Asia, south of the Aral Sea. Khiva was famed for its ivory workers, who manufactured magnificent sword and dagger handles and exquisitely carved ornaments from arctic ivory and sold them to Persia, Baghdad and Egypt. Narwhal and walrus ivory came from Siberia's northern coast. The source of most mammoth tusks was the Berezovo district of Siberia, a region particularly rich in mammoth remains. There archeologists have found silver vessels with 12th-century Kufic inscriptions, probably bartered ages ago for arctic ivory. (When my wife and I retraced some of the ancient ivory routes in the spring of 1989, we had no luck at all in Bukhara and Samarkand. The memory and all traces of the long-ago ivory trade had vanished. However, in Khiva an old man recalled that in the time of the khans a palace door had been covered with gold, coral and ivory. After a long search we found the door. It had long ago been stripped of gold and coral and most of the ivory platelets were gone, but a few remained, dark brown with dirt and age. After cleaning them, I identified with a thrill their unmistakable twist. In this remote oasis of Central Asia, they had been carved many centuries ago from the tusk of the arctic narwhal.)

The fourth route—really a complex network of routes—brought arctic ivory in trade and tribute, transported from tribe to tribe by dog teams, reindeer sleds, pack horses and Bactrian camels, from the north Siberian coast and the Chukchi Peninsula to China, with a branchline that extended northeast into Alaska at least a thousand years before Columbus discovered America.

Nearly all *ku-tu-si*, the narwhal tusks metamorphosed into unicorn horns, remained in China. Nobles who paid for their exalted state with a constant fear of being poisoned, bought the horns as a sort of extremely expensive life insurance, and since unicorn horns were considered sacred in China, many were also kept in temples. But a few horns along with their name, shortened to *khutu* in Arabic, traveled from China along that 4,000-mile east-west conduit of luxury products known as the Silk Road via Samarkand and Bukhara to Baghdad, Tyre, Constantinople and Alexandria. "The Egyptians crave [unicorn horn]," wrote the Arab historian al-Biruni (973–1048), because ". . . the approach of poison causes it to exude." The farther a narwhal's tusk traveled, the greater its price and fame. By the time such a tusk reached Egypt, said al-Biruni, it was "two hundred times" more expensive than in China. Occasionally a faint glimmer of truth touched the fantastic tales that surrounded unicorn horns. A 1073 Turkish-Arabic dictionary defined *khutu* as the "horn of a sea fish imported from China . . . It is used for knife handles. The presence of poison in the food is put to the test by it."

In China and Japan the implicit faith in the unicorn and its miraculous horn lasted for thousands of years and continued long after its glory had dimmed in the West, where the horns had been exposed as tusks of an arctic whale and demoted from precious treasures of gullible princes to fancy walking sticks of the bourgeoisie. In addition to tusks from Siberia, China and especially Japan found a new source of unicorn horn — Greenland and, later, the Canadian Arctic. The middlemen were mainly Dutch.

The Dutch were the master mariners of the 17th century. Amsterdam in 1700 was Europe's most important port and the wealthiest city in the world. The Dutch owned the world's greatest whaling fleet and sailed each year to the Arctic. To the intense annoyance of the Danes, who claimed Greenland, the Dutch traded extensively with Greenland Inuit and sold their furs, whale oil and narwhal tusks in Europe and Japan. They began the trade with Japan in 1567, at first in competition with Spaniards and Portuguese. In 1637 an increasingly xenophobic Japanese government banned all foreigners except Dutch traders who were confined to De-Jima Island in Nagasaki harbor. The Dutch

"The Japanese have an extravagant opinion of [the unicorn horn's] medical virtues and powers to prolong life, fortify the animal spirits, assist the memory, and cure all complaints."

— CHARLES PETER THUNBERG, English botanist and traveler, 1775

The narwhal's tusk, long believed to be merely the symbol of the male, like a lion's mane, is now thought to be a weapon that males use in dominance disputes. Flip Nicklin

A tusked male narwhal upon an arctic beach.

The Swedish bishop Olaus Magnus shows a fierce "sea unicorn" on a map published in Venice in 1539.

brought to wealthy but isolated Japan glass and mirrors, camphor, spectacles, chintz, watches and "unicorn horns."

The immensely lucrative trade in unicorn horns began in the late 18th century when a trader brought to Japan a collection of curios, among them a narwhal tusk from Greenland. The Japanese were ecstatic; here was a genuine unicorn horn. They paid such a fortune for it, the fortunate Dutchman retired, wealthy for the rest of his life. The Japanese, noted the English botanist and traveler Charles Peter Thunberg, who visited Nagasaki in 1775, "have an extravagant opinion of [the unicorn horn's] medical virtues and powers to prolong life, fortify the animal spirits, assist the memory and cure all complaints." The Inuit, at the production end of this extraordinary trade route, learned early that of all things their land and sea produced, it was narwhal tusks that white traders most desired. On July 7, 1652, the Dutch ship *St. Peter* anchored in Itivdleq Fiord on Greenland's west coast and, noted the captain in his logbook, Inuit in kayaks "immediately came quite close and shouted 'tuacha,' which is unicorn . . ." (*tûgaq* is the modern Greenlandic word for narwhal tusk).

The oriental demand for unicorn horns continued into the 19th and 20th centuries. In 1868 the British naturalist Robert Brown wrote that "the price of Narwhal's ivory . . . of late years . . . has risen prodigiously in value owing to the repair of Chinese palaces." The geologist A.P. Low led a Canadian government expedition to Pond Inlet on Baffin Island in 1903 and found that narwhal tusks were the main item of Inuit trade. "The ultimate destination of the [narwhal] ivory is China," Low wrote, "where it is used for ornamental purposes as well as for medicine, and for the manufacture of cups supposed to absorb all poisons placed into them." In this century Pond Inlet became the center of the narwhal hunt. In 1923, the Hudson's Bay Company manager at Pond Inlet reported to his superiors, "The Narwhal industry has been developed . . . almost to its limit . . . Five or six hundred Narwhal would be considered as only an ordinary year's hunt."

The hunt and the demand for narwhal tusks continues, ancient legends linger. In 1981 two of Canada's foremost sea mammal specialists, Edward Mitchell and Randall R. Reeves, found their research into the use of narwhal ivory hampered because suppliers were reluctant to divulge details of how they obtained narwhal tusks and to whom they sold them. They did, however, discover that many tusks were sent to Japan. There, "pulverized or turned into shavings, narwhal ivory was sold as the wonder drug *ikkaku* . . . as recently as the 1950s."

THE NARWHAL'S REALM

Three whale species live in the circumpolar arctic seas: the bowhead, a ponderous and placid giant; the beluga, as gleaming white as arctic ice; and its close cousin, the tusked, elusive narwhal.

The bowhead, or Greenland right whale, is a huge, lumbering animal with a gigantic head, a mouth the size of a large living room, and flukes 24 feet wide. Adults are 40 to 60 feet long and can weigh up to 60 tons, yet they feed on animals so small, they must consume daily 15 to 30 million tiny shrimplike euphausiids and copepods, and pteropods, small winged pelagic snails. In summer, when the arctic seas are aswarm with life, the whales swim leisurely through this broth and scoop up "brit," as whalers called the massed crustaceans and snails. When a whale has a mouthful, its one-ton tongue moves up, the water gushes out through the latticework of baleen, and the retained animal gruel is pressed back and swallowed, at least one ton each day.

Bowheads were called "right whales" because they were the right ones to hunt: slow and timid, swathed in 30 tons of blubber, their cavernous mouths filled with valuable baleen. The mild-mannered giants were slaughtered for centuries until few remained. About 300 are left in the immensity of the eastern Arctic, and about 5,000 in the west.

I watched their fall migration late one evening from a hill on Herschel Island in Canada's Beaufort Sea, once headquarters of western Arctic whalers. Twin plumes of exhaled breath hung briefly in the faint light of the dying day as they slowly swam past the island, the last survivors of a mighty tribe.

The white whale or beluga (a name derived from the Russian word *belyi*, "white") is gregarious and garrulous, the most vocal of all whales. Because belugas often whistle, sailors called them "sea canaries." Narwhal and beluga are the only members of the *Monodontidae* family. They are similar in size and weight, both lack dorsal fins—an adaptation to life among ice—and both live in the arctic seas. But whereas adult belugas are pure white, narwhals are strangely mottled; belugas like the shallows, narwhals prefer deep water; solitary belugas may wander far (to the Mediterranean, for example), narwhals rarely stray; and belugas of both sexes have about 40 short, blunt, peglike teeth, while in narwhals the female has no teeth at all and the male has only one, the famous spiraled tusk. (In that rare and charming 17th-century book *Histoire*

Above: *The elegant harp seals spend summers in the far northern seas and migrate south in fall, ahead of the advancing ice.*

Opposite: *Glowing in the Arctic's midnight sun, an iceberg drifts along Eclipse Sound, Baffin Island.*

Naturelle et Morale des Iles Antilles, César de Rochefort devotes, in an odd aside, an entire chapter to Inuit and narwhals and argues that the narwhal, having expended "all the tooth-making material" of his body on that one magnificent tusk, has none left for any other teeth.)

White whales often summer in estuaries and shallow bays. Ten thousand gather in Canada's Mackenzie River delta, about 2,000 congregate in the estuaries of the Churchill and Seal rivers on the west coast of Hudson Bay, and 1,000 mass in Somerset Island's Cunningham Inlet in Canada's High Arctic, where I watched them during three enchanted summers with scientists from Canada's Arctic Biological Station.

I sat on a hill overlooking the inlet in mid-July when the belugas arrived. They surged through the cool green water like gleaming, ivory-white torpedoes, their heart-shaped flukes rising and falling in smooth rhythm, glittering bow waves curling against their heads. Dark-hued calves swarm like small shadows near their massive white mothers. One whale rose from the depth with a long frond of seaweed in its mouth. Others rushed towards it, joyfully nipping at the frond until the trophy was in tatters. The belugas were playful and noisy. On windless days we heard their squeaks and whistles at our camp, more than a mile from the inlet and wondered what the whales were "talking" about.

The white whales of the North fare well. Once heavily hunted, they have recovered. North America's white whale population now numbers about 50,000 and an equal or perhaps larger number inhabits the seas north of the former Soviet Union. But one beluga group, an Ice Age relic population in the St. Lawrence River estuary and the Gulf of St. Lawrence, faces extinction.

During the Pleistocene, white whales, narwhals and walruses ranged much further south than they do today. Fossil narwhal bones are common in the so-called "Forest Bed" in Norfolk, England, laid down in the early Pleistocene, nearly two million years ago. Ten thousand years ago, near the end of the Pleistocene, that vast ocean arm known as the Champlain Sea extended from the Atlantic inland far beyond today's Lake Ontario. Its icy waters were home to belugas, narwhals and walruses. Their skeletons have been found near Montreal and Rivière-du-Loup in Quebec and Burlington in Ontario.

As the sea became warmer, narwhals retreated to the Far North, but populations of walruses and belugas remained in the south. After the European discovery of Canada, the great walrus herds in the Gulf of St. Lawrence were relentlessly hunted (the last walrus there was killed in 1799) for their blubber, their thick hides and especially for their ivory tusks. The tusks brought high prices in Europe after Alexander Woodson of Bristol, a prominent 16th-century physician, tested the ivory and "found it as soveraigne against poyson as any Unicornes horne." The belugas, too, were intensively hunted. Bootlaces were made from their hides, "and nothing exceeds it for covering coaches," wrote the Jesuit priest Pierre de Charlevoix in 1720. Now the St. Lawrence belugas

Whales were once so numerous near the Norwegian coast that "the sea looks like a great city with its chimneys smoking."

— PONTOPPIDAN, Bishop of Bergen, Norway, 18th century

THE NARWHAL'S REALM   33

About one walrus in a thousand is a "killer," a rogue that feeds primarily on seals and on very rare occasions may kill a narwhal.

Herring gull on wave-washed rocks at sunset. Opportunistic, pushy and abundant, these gulls thrive in the south and also in the Far North.

A furious hooded seal mother defends her newborn pup. Nursed frequently, hooded seal pups gain about 15 pounds each day and are weaned after four days, the shortest lactation period known for any mammal.

A polar bear and its reflection on the new-formed ice of Hudson Bay.

are protected, but their river is so severely polluted that the poisons are slowly killing the whales. The last 500 seem doomed.

Narwhals are whales of the ice. In its leads, ponds and ice-shielded bays, they seek sanctuary from the killer whale, the enemy they most fear, and their vast annual migrations follow the seasonal rhythm of advancing and retreating ice. On July 30, 1980, the sea mammal specialist Wybrand Hoek and I were flying above the still-frozen Peel Sound in Canada's High Arctic, when we suddenly came upon a broad lead, an ink-black gash of open water between the gleaming ice. In it lay more than 1,000 narwhals (unlike other whales, narwhals may lie at or near the surface, sometimes for hours). There were groups of females and calves, and groups of males, some in rosettes, all tusks pointed towards the center, and others that seemed to roll and joust and spar in a strange fluid sea ballet.

After decades of intensive study, our knowledge of narwhals, of their range and migrations, is still sketchy. The world's 20,000 to 30,000 narwhals inhabit an area larger than Europe, and they live in the least visited, most inaccessible seas. Even extensive aerial surveys can be misleading. The day we saw the massed narwhals in Peel Sound, we had already flown for 12 hours. Although we had skirted the ice edge, flown over sheltered bays and quartered an area larger than Holland, we had seen only 14 narwhals in a region where they are supposed to be common in summer. Then, suddenly, came that marvelous thrill —more than a thousand narwhals at their ease in one broad band of open water among the vastness of the ice. Had we flown five miles further east or west we would have missed this concentration and could have concluded that, at least this summer, narwhals were rare in that region.

Narwhals are now, according to the Russian cetologist A.V. Yablokov, "extremely rare" in the seas north of the former Soviet Union. Yet once they were common in this region which, for thousands of years, supplied most of China's "unicorn horns." As the *Fram*, the ship of the Norwegian explorer Fridtjof Nansen, drifted with the ice across the Arctic Ocean north of Siberia in 1895 and 1896, its crew was often amazed "that there should be so many narwhals in the lanes here." On July 22, 1895, in the ice at 84°53′N, between Franz Josef Land and the North Pole, they saw "seven or eight female narwhals gambolling in the channel near" the ship and later that day "the lane swarmed with whales . . ."

The Swedish explorer N.A. Nordenskiöld, who conquered the Northeast Passage in 1878–79, saw few narwhals but reported that another scientist, Witsen, had seen large "herds" between Spitsbergen and Novaya Zemlya. Whalers were active in this region for centuries. They killed thousands of bowheads but rarely pursued narwhals. Friedrich Martens, a wealthy Hamburg businessman, visited the "whale fishery" in Spitsbergen in 1671, where, at nearly 80°N, only 700 miles from the North Pole, the Dutch had built a whaling village. Aptly

"The Sea-Unicorn is known to frequent Hudson's Bay and straits . . ."

— SAMUEL HEARNE, British explorer, 1789

Narwhals "prefer the proximity of ice, probably to escape the attacks of the giant Killer [whale] . . ."

— ALFRED TREMBLAY, Canadian trader, 1910

named Smeerenburg ("Blubberburg"), it contained extensive tryworks where blubber was rendered into oil, as well as taverns, a church, a bakery and a bordello. "The Unicorn," reported Martens, was not hunted because "this fish swims with such great speed that, although they are seen, they are rarely taken." Russian scientists are now certain that narwhals are rare in these seas but no one knows what has caused their decline.

Along northeast Asia and Alaska narwhals are so rare (less than a dozen have been seen near Alaska in the last 100 years), the few sightings have led to fabulous reports that one of the strangest animals of the north, the long-extinct Steller's sea cow, may still exist. This gigantic subarctic cousin of the tropical and subtropical manatee and dugong, was first seen by the Russian expedition headed by Vitus Bering near the Commander Islands in the southwest Bering Sea in 1741. These 8,000-pound animals, with skins like the bark of ancient oaks, were placidly munching seaweed in the coastal shallows. Their curse was to be slow and meek and to taste like the finest veal. The last of these gentle giants was reportedly killed in 1768. Then Nordenskiöld, stopping at the Commander Islands on his way home in 1879 after traversing the Northeast Passage, was told by residents they had seen a sea cow. The scientist Leonard Steyneger rushed to the remote islands, interviewed the people and concluded sadly "their description exactly fits the female narwhal." In 1963 hopes were again raised that the Steller's sea cow might still live. Soviet whalers in the Bering Sea claimed to have seen it. But when scientists pressed them for details, it quickly became obvious that what they had seen had been a narwhal. The narwhal still visits these seas, though rarely; the sea cow is extinct.

Although a discrete and little-known population of about 4,000 narwhals exists in the seas off the ice-girt east Greenland coast, the vast majority live in Davis Strait and Baffin Bay, between Greenland and Baffin Island, and in adjacent straits, sounds and bays. William Baffin saw them in 1616, 200 years before John Ross, when he took the *Discovery* (the stout little ship that had already carried Henry Hudson to Hudson Bay in 1610) along the west Greenland coast into the great bay that now bears his name. He met Inuit and they gave him "many peeces of bone or horne of the sea unicorne." In late June Baffin started to see "the fishes with long hornes, many and often, which we call the sea unicorne . . ." and later he wrote to his backer, Sir John Wolstenholme, "As for the sea-unicorne . . . if the horne be of any good value, no doubt but many of them may be killed." The whales of this still pristine region were tame, he said, "because they are not used to be chased."

The whales were spared for 200 years until in 1818 Ross led the whalers into Baffin Bay and in 1819 William Edward Parry sailed into Lancaster Sound, "the headquarters of the whales." From whalers' observations and later those of scientists, a picture gradually emerged of a great annual north-south narwhal migration. On September 7, 1939, the Danish biologist Christian Vibe saw

Gregarious and garrulous, belugas mass in summer near the estuaries of some northern rivers.

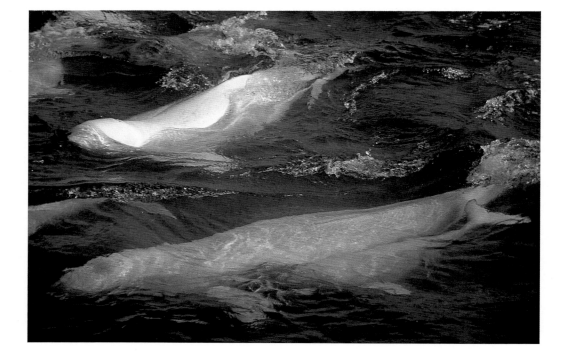

The beluga or white whale of the North is the narwhal's closest relative.

A curious beluga "spyhops." Pushing itself forward and upward with its powerful fluke, the whale rises partly out of the water for a better look.

near Inglefield Bay in northwest Greenland "... a large-scale Narwhal migration. Flocks of some twenty animals, males and females together, were seen passing closely at intervals of a few minutes. It was an impressive sight ... The whole migration lasted for an hour and then about 1000 Narwhals had passed by." In the same area in 1984, the Danish scientist Erik W. Born saw "on several days, herds of more than 3,000 ... and on August 18 a single herd numbering 4,043 narwhals was counted."

On July 10, 1957, the Canadian ornithologist Leslie M. Tuck, studying murres high on Bylot Island's Cape Hay, watched the great migration of narwhals. They passed in small groups at the rate of 250 to 300 an hour, about 2,500 in one day, all bound for Lancaster Sound. Nineteen years later, the Canadian biologist R.G. Greendale and his wife spent six weeks atop the same limestone cliff, a thousand feet above the sea, and counted the sea mammals that passed: 8 polar bears, 23 bowhead whales, 83 walruses, 168 bearded seals, 132,000 harp seals and 6,145 narwhals. Since it was often foggy and visibility poor, the Greendales estimated that 8,000 to 10,000 narwhals had migrated from Baffin Bay around Cape Hay into Lancaster Sound.

Slowly the pieces of the puzzle fell into place. The narwhals did not winter in the North Water, that great polynya in Baffin Bay, as had been assumed until recently, but, according to Erik Born, in the heavy pack ice in northern Davis Strait and southern Baffin Bay. In March about 1,400 narwhals swim towards Hudson Bay. The other narwhals swim slowly northward, feeding and following the receding ice. In late June they reach northern Baffin Island. About 1,000 to 2,000 bunch near Pond Inlet, another 2,000 swim into Admiralty Inlet, and about 15,000 migrate through Lancaster Sound to summer in that maze of bays, sounds and channels among the High Arctic Canadian islands. Four thousand or more swim north and east to spend summer in the great Inglefield Bay of northwest Greenland, amid drifting ice fields and the thunder and surge of calving glaciers. Some swim into Kane Basin between Ellesmere Island and Greenland, and a few may venture even further north, right into the Arctic Ocean. Russian scientists on drift-ice stations have seen narwhals less than 200 miles from the North Pole.

Unlike belugas, few swim far to the south. White whales with wanderlust end up in the oddest places. One spent the spring of 1972 in Buzzards Bay, Massachusetts; another swam along the southern coast of France. The most famous white whale of all was one that swam up the Rhine in 1966. It became the sensation of Europe. Promptly, but misleadingly, dubbed Moby Dick (the white whale of Herman Melville's famous novel was an albino sperm whale), the beluga leisurely ascended the river past Düsseldorf, Cologne and Bonn, while excursion boats milled about and thousands of people watched from the riverbank. The whale spent a month in the Rhine and then returned to the sea.

Narwhals rarely leave their arctic realm. During the past five centuries, seven

"Narwhals come into Pond's Inlet and Eclipse Sound as soon as the ice breaks ..."

— JOSEPH ELZÉAR BERNIER, Canadian explorer, 1907

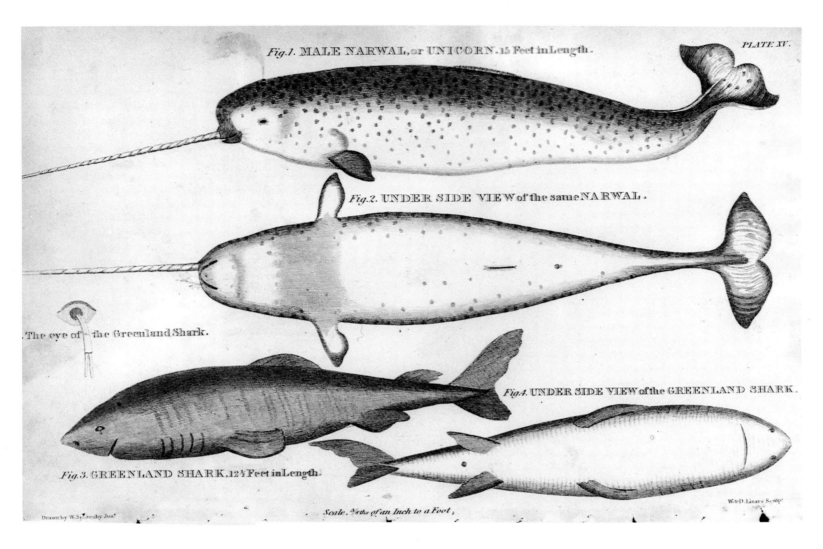

Illustrations of "Male Narwhal or Unicorn" and "Greenland Shark" from An Account of the Arctic Regions *by the famous whaling captain William Scoresby.* Metropolitan Toronto Library Board

narwhals have been found on the coast of Norway, one in Holland, two in Germany and six in Great Britain. The last two in Britain were both 13-foot females found stranded in 1949, one in the Thames estuary not far from London. Most famous was the 1648 stranding of a large, tusked male upon the Island of May in Scotland's Firth of Forth. It was studied and dissected by the scientist Tulpius, who named it the *Unicornis marinum*.

Ice is the smooth-backed narwhal's protector. It shields it from the tall-finned killer whale. The trader Alfred Tremblay watched the whales near Pond Inlet in the summer of 1910. The narwhals, he observed "usually travel in bands and appear to prefer the proximity of the ice, probably to escape the attacks of the giant Killer which pursues it relentlessly." If there is no ice, narwhals may dash into shallow water in a desperate attempt to evade the fast killer whales. Researchers John Ford and Deborah Cavanagh were recording underwater sounds in Koluktoo Bay in 1985, when suddenly 12 killer whales appeared. "As soon as the killer whales began vocalizing under water, all narwhal calls ceased," Ford and Cavanagh reported. "The five hundred or more narwhals in the bay became extremely agitated and crowded into the shallows."

*Spitsbergen, north of Norway, was the center
of the centuries-long hunt by Dutch, British
and German whalers.*

An arctic tern upon a boulder covered with a bright orange nitrophilous lichen that thrives on bird droppings. Champion migrants, these terns breed in the Far North, then fly as far south as Antarctica.

Black guillemots nest in rock crevices and feed primarily on benthic fish and crustaceans, usually near shore.

The explorer-writer Peter Freuchen claimed that often two killer whales will swim on either side of a fleeing narwhal "then press the unfortunate smaller whale between them with such force that all his ribs break." The killer whales continue the hunt and return later to eat the crippled animal. Masautsiaq, the Polar Inuk of northwest Greenland with whom I lived for many months, said he had seen a killer whale ram a narwhal with such force, the 3,000-pound animal was lifted clear out of the water. Killer whales seem to fear only one animal, the walrus. When a Polar Inuk is hunting in his kayak and is surprised far from shore by killer whales, he cups his hands and bellows into the water, imitating the roar of an enraged walrus bull. The sound travels far in the water, and Masautsiaq told me that the killer whales promptly veer off.

On rare occasions, a walrus may kill a narwhal. Most walruses are harmless shellfish eaters. But about one in a thousand is a "killer," a rogue that feeds on seals and other marine mammals. Such rogues are waifs, say Inuit, animals that lost their mothers while still young. First they feed on carrion, then develop a taste for meat and begin to kill and eat seals. The appearance of such rogues is distinctive. The shoulders and forelimbs appear unusually large and powerfully developed. Chin, throat, chest and tusks are amber colored by oxydized seal oil. Their tusks tend to be long, slender and sharp, twin ivory stilettos. A rogue walrus, say the Inuit, swims quietly up to a sleeping seal, enfolds it with its powerful front flippers, crushes it, rips the skin with his tusks, eats the intestines, and sucks off the blubber and some of the meat. Such rogues take mainly seals, but when the chance presents itself, they use the same technique to surprise, kill and eat a narwhal. The famous English whaling skipper Robert Gray, on a voyage in the Norwegian Sea in 1890, noticed ". . . something floating in greasy water surrounded by birds . . . it proved to be a dead narwhal. It was criss-crossed with wounds and its abdominal viscera had been eaten away. The culprit, a large walrus, was asleep on a neighboring piece of ice."

Hans Egede, the 18th-century "Apostle of Greenland," writing in his usual lapidary, matter-of-fact style said about the Greenland shark that "it is a fish of prey, bites large pieces out of the whale's body, and is very greedy after man's flesh." The only shark of the Arctic, it is primarily a carrion eater; whenever there is death in northern seas, this shark is sure to appear. Polar Inuit were cutting up narwhals in shallow water near our camp at Inglefield Bay in northwest Greenland when a great shark slid silently across the pebbles and sliced chunks from one of the whales. Children threw rocks at it; it paid no heed. The men finally shot it, but the dying shark kept eating, driven by greed.

Sharks, walruses, even killer whales are minor threats. The narwhal's main enemy is man. Once, very long ago, arctic men hunted narwhals solely as food and used the tusks for tools or carved children's toys from them. Later, some tusks traveled south by long and complex routes, their origin a secret, and became, in time, the shining, spiraled horns of unicorns.

"As for the sea-unicorne . . . if the horne be of any good value, no doubt but many of them may be killed."

— WILLIAM BAFFIN, English arctic explorer, 1616

Whales "are after a fashion land and water animals in one."

— ARISTOTLE, Greek philosopher, 384–322 BC

On rare occasions, polar bears will catch narwhals trapped by ice in a savssat.

OF UNICORNS AND VIRGINS

Ctesias of Cnidus was a physician, his father was a physician, his grandfather was a physician, and he claimed descent from Asclepius, the Greek god of medicine. He was so famous in his time that in 416 BC he was appointed court physician to Darius II, king of Persia, and to his successor, Artaxerxes. He served them faithfully for 18 years, returned to Greece a wealthy man and wrote about the wonders he had seen and heard in his 20-volume *Persica*.

In India, Ctesias had been told by merchants, there are "certain wild asses as large as horses, and larger . . . They have a horn on the forehead which is about a foot and a half in length. The dust filed from this horn is administered in a potion as a protection against deadly drugs . . . Those who drink out of these horns, made into drinking vessels, are not subject, they say, to convulsions and to the holy disease [epilepsy]. Indeed, they are immune even to poison if, either before or after swallowing such, they drink wine, water, or anything else from these beakers." And thus did the unicorn and the legend of its wonder-working horn come to Europe.

Aristotle, who lived shortly after Ctesias (from 384–322 BC), did not think highly of his tales, but he did accept the unicorn. After all, a people who believed in the phoenix, a bird that burned itself every 500 years and then rose brand-new from the ashes, did not find it difficult to believe in unicorns with magic horns. (Flame-red phoenix feathers were sold in medieval markets; most were flamingo feathers.) Aristotle, who devoted entire chapters to such birds as the wryneck and the hoopoe, said little about the unicorn. He pointed out that most horned animals have two horns, then added, "Still, there are some that have but a single horn; the Oryx, for instance, and the so-called Indian ass . . . in such animals the horn is set in the center of the head." Nevertheless, the mere fact that Aristotle mentioned the unicorn gave it a lasting reality.

To the Greeks and later the Romans, the unicorn was merely a biological oddity. Naturalists such as Pliny and Aelian described it long and learnedly, but it never caught the public fancy, as had the giraffe, for instance. The giraffe was brought to Rome through the empire's vast network of animal dealers and was described by some as the "camelopard," the offspring, it was said, of that most unlikely of unions between a camel and a leopard. But at least the giraffe was produced; the unicorn remained mythical. As the Swiss naturalist Konrad

Above: *Beguiled by a naked maiden, the blissful unicorn is easy prey for the evil hunter. Detail of a 13th-century miniature in an English bestiary.* The British Library

Opposite: *The unicorn is Christ in this detail from the famous painting* Madonna and Unicorn *by the artist known as the Spanish Forger.* The Pierpont Morgan Library

von Gesner pointed out in 1551, "while Roman pomp knew how to bring all animals to their triumphal marches, one nowhere reads that a unicorn was ever shown to the Roman people."

That, really, was not true. Romans had frequently seen unicorns; they simply did not realize it. The finest of the classical unicorn descriptions, all based on Ctesias, was written by Julius Solinus in his *Polyhistoria*, beautifully translated by Arthur Golding in 1587: "But the cruellest [of all animals] is the Unicorne . . . bodyed like a horse, footed like an Eliphant, tayled like a Swyne, and headed like a Stagge. His horne sticketh out of the midds of hys forehead, of a wonderful brightness about foure foote long, so sharp, that whatsoever he push-eth at, he striketh it through easily. He is never caught alive; kylled he may be, but taken he cannot bee." The animal Ctesias and his successors described as *monoceros*, the horned ass of India, was the rhinoceros so often seen in Roman parades, yet it never seems to have occurred to anyone that the two were one and the same animal.

The Greeks and Romans never depicted the unicorn, and no mention is made in any Roman account of trade in the unicorn's poison-defeating horn. Perhaps demand was not as acute as it would be later in human history. In Greece and Rome the art of poisoning was not as highly developed nor as widely applied as in the East and later in Europe. Roman and Greek assassins usually opted for the direct approach—the dagger or the sword.

Two events changed the unicorn's status from that of a strange beast in the remote East, to an animal of great beauty, sanctity and mystic power. The first was the rise of Christianity and with it the Bible, in which the unicorn is mentioned seven times, thus giving it divine recognition. The second was the publication in Alexandria in the 2nd century of an infallible recipe for captur-ing unicorns—use virgins as bait. That caught everyone's attention.

In about 250 BC, when the 72 scholars of Alexandria who, according to tradition, translated the Old Testament from Hebrew into Greek, came to the word *re'em*, they were momentarily stymied. It evidently denoted a mighty animal of great power. It meant, in fact, the now extinct urus or aurochs, *Bos primigenius*, the wild ox of Eurasia and North Africa, ancestor of most European domestic cattle. (The last one died in 1627 in the Jaktorow Forest near Warsaw, Poland.) Unlike those who wrote the Old Testament, its translators were city people and not pastoralists, and they knew little about cattle, wild or domestic. But they had heard reports of the power of the unicorn and therefore translated *re'em* as *monoceros*, "the mighty unicorn," as in: "God brought them out of Egypt; he hath as it were the strength of an unicorn" (Numbers 23:22), or "But my horn shalt thou exalt like the horn of an unicorn" (Psalm 92:11). And so the unicorn became holy writ and to question its existence was tantamount to blasphemy.

In the 2nd century, an unknown author in Alexandria penned a slim book

The unicorn "has a stag's head, elephant's feet, and a boar's tail, the rest of the body being like that of a horse."

— PLINY THE ELDER, Roman naturalist, 23–79

The unicorn's all-healing horn was a symbol of the medical and pharmaceutical profession. This unicorn with its narwhal tusk graced an ancient Einhornapotheke, *a German apothecary shop.* Germanisches National Museum, Nürnberg

that became known as the *Physiologus* ("The Naturalist"). Each short chapter began with a quotation from Scripture, followed by "Physiologus says . . ." and then a fanciful fable; for instance, the long-lived tale that the pelican stabs his breast and feeds the blood to his young. The *Physiologus* was one of the great best-sellers of all time. It went through countless editions for more than a thousand years, was translated into many languages — among them Syriac, Norse, Armenian, Anglo-Saxon and Provençal — and was parent to the *Bestiaries*, the immensely popular moralistic animal tales of the Middle Ages. The unicorn, Physiologus says, is swift and wild and can never be caught by hunters. Then he tells "how it is captured. A virgin is placed before it and it springs into the virgin's lap and she warms it with love and carries it off to the palace of kings."

There was another ancient method of catching unicorns. The "Valiant Little Tailor" uses it in the Grimms' fairy-tale. To win the princess, he must, among other valorous deeds, capture a unicorn that roams the forest and "does great harm." Using himself as bait, the little tailor stands in front of a tree. As the

The unicorn dips its miracle-working horn into a stream in the Garden of Eden and purifies the water so all animals can drink of it. Detail of an altarpiece by Hieronymus Bosch, early 16th century. Copyright Museo del Prado, Madrid

"This unicorn is Christ whose might, typefied by its horn, is irresistible."

— SAINT ALBERTUS MAGNUS, scholastic philospher, 1193–1280

unicorn charges, he leaps nimbly aside, the animal's horn goes deeply into the wood and thus the unicorn is caught.

Hunters also obtained the precious spiraled horn in this way, wrote the Elizabethan poet Edmund Spenser (1552–99). The hunter stands in front of a tree:

> And when him running in full course he spies,
> He slips aside; the whiles that furious beast
> His precious horn, sought of his enimies,
> Strikes in the strocke, ne thence can be releast.

Lions knew the trick. "Wherefore as soon as a lion sees an unicorn, he runneth to a tree for succor," said the fabulist Edward Topsell in 1658, and Shakespeare, too, knew "that unicorns may be betray'd with trees" (*Julius Caesar* II:1).

While this method of capturing unicorns required, no doubt, ingenuity, courage and skill, it could not hope to compete with the virgin method, which had much wider appeal. The story was lovingly enhanced and embroidered. The haughty abbess Hildegard of Bingen, one of the great mystics of the 12th century, declared that as unicorn bait not just any plump peasant virgin would do. It had to be a girl of noble birth, who was virginal, beautiful and enticing. But, the abbess warned, to cheat a unicorn meant death. If a girl was not truly a virgin, the unicorn would sense it and in furious anger transfix her with his horn.

Some of the greatest minds were fascinated by unicorns. Leonardo da Vinci wrote a treatise on how to capture them: "In its lack of moderation and restraint and the predilection it has for young girls, it completely forgets its shyness and wildness; it puts aside all distrust, goes up to the sitting girl and falls asleep in her lap. In this way hunters catch it."

The waiting girl becomes seductress; she allures, entraps and betrays the unicorn, her lover. It was a theme of immense popularity in poems, ballads and songs. Thibaut IV (1201–53), poet, trouvère and king of Navarre (among his many titles he was also Count of Champagne and Brie) likened himself to the unicorn:

> The unicorn and I are one:
> He also pauses in amaze
> Before some maiden's magic gaze,
> And while he wonders, is undone,
> On some dear breast he slumbers deep
> And Treason slays him in that sleep.
> Just so have ended my Life's days;
> So Love and my Lady lay me low.
> My heart will not survive this blow.

In the spirit of the times, the story could by turns be deliciously erotic, the shining horn a symbol of power and vitality, or, in one of those odd twists the medieval mind seemed to delight in, the unicorn could also stand for Christ and the horn for His power. "Who is this unicorn but the only begotten son of God?" declaimed Saint Ambrose, bishop of Milan (340–397). Saint Basil the Great, bishop of Caesarea in Cappadocia (330–379), explained, "Christ is the power of God, therefore He is called the unicorn on the ground that He has one horn, that is, one common power with the Father." In many medieval paintings, the Virgin Mary holds a unicorn as she might hold the infant Jesus.

Somehow medieval man had no problem in imbuing the unicorn, his favorite animal, with these wildly contradictory attributes. It stood for power and virtue, for earthly love and heavenly love, for freedom that could not be shackled and wildness that could not be bound; it stood for might and right, for valor and nobility and, in a darker guise, it stood for doom and death. It is therefore not surprising that with all these marvelous attributes the unicorn became a favorite animal of artists and of heraldry. It underwent many metamorphoses and over the ages changed from the elephant-footed, swine-tailed clod of Solinus to the gallant steed with a shining horn that purifies poisoned water in Hieronymus Bosch's *Garden of Earthly Delights*. One thing, though, most unicorns have in common, whether it is the cuddly unicorn of Raphael, the powerful unicorn of Hans Holbein, the sensual unicorns of Gustave Moreau, the haltered unicorn sketched by Leonardo da Vinci, or the hundreds and thousands of unicorns other artists portrayed: they all carry a horn that is unmistakably a narwhal tusk, the only long, spiraled horn in all creation.

This horn is borne by the unicorn that supports Britain's Royal Coat of Arms. While the lion represented England, the Scottish kings had chosen the unicorn, symbol of prowess and courage, as their emblem, and the popular nursery rhyme

The Lion and the Unicorn
Were fighting for the Crown;
The Lion chased the Unicorn
All around the town.

started life as a political ditty about the rivalry between England and Scotland. Edmund Spenser in *The Faerie Queene* alluded to the same rivalry when he wrote: "Like as a Lyon whose imperiall powre/A proud rebellious Unicorn defyes." Scottish kings even minted gold coins that carried the unicorn image and were known as "unicorn" and "half-unicorn." When James VI of Scotland became King James I of England in 1603, he took the Scottish unicorn along, bumped the red griffin of Wales, and ever since the Royal Coat of Arms, in the marvelous language of heraldry, has been supported dexter by "A lion rampant,

"From his stately forehead springs, Piercing to heaven, a radiant horn! Lo, the compeer of lion-kings, The steed self-armed, the Unicorn."

— GEORGE DARLEY, Irish poet, 1835

Because of the unicorn's "predilection . . . for young girls, it completely forgets its shyness and wildness . . . it goes up to the sitting girl and falls asleep in her lap."

— LEONARDO DA VINCI, 1452–1519. Advice for unicorn catchers.

gardant . . ." and sinister by "a unicorn argent, armed, crined, and unguled . . ."

All the symbolism, the beauty and the legends of the unicorn come together, as in no other work of art, in the seven magnificent *Unicorn Tapestries* now in The Cloisters in New York. In them, the unicorn, snow-white and with a spiraled horn, dips his magic horn into a stream to rid it of poison. It is lured to its death by a maiden and killed by evil men with brutal executioners' faces. Finally, the resurrected unicorn, a symbol of Christ and immortality, lies in a field of flowers, surrounded by a fence and tied by a *chaine d'amour* to a pomegranate tree.

The unicorn was often depicted in art, but seldom seen. Its existence had to be taken largely on faith. Julius Caesar in *The Gallic War* reported matter-of-factly that the unicorn roamed the immense Hercynian forest of central Europe and that it was "shaped like a stag, from the middle of whose forehead, between the ears, stands forth a single horn, taller and straighter than the horns we know." Many sightings were edifyingly linked to Bible stories. The Dutch priest Johannes van Hesse of Utrecht went on a pilgrimage to Palestine in 1389. There, "near the field of Helyon in the Promised Land is the river Marah, whose bitter waters Moses made sweet with a stroke from his staff and the children of Israel drank thereof (Exodus: 23:25). To this day, it is said, malicious animals poison this water after sundown . . . But early in the morning, as soon as the sun rises, a unicorn comes out of the ocean, dips his horn into the stream and drives out the venom from it so that the other animals may drink thereof during the day." And this, he assures us, "I saw with my own eyes."

Not everyone believed in unicorns, and the French satirist François Rabelais (1490–1553) even poked ribald fun at it. He wrote about a journey to the Land of Satin. "I saw there two-and-twenty unicorns. They are a cursed sort of creature, much resembling a fine horse, unless it be that their heads are like a stag's, their feet like an elephant's, their tails like a wild boar's, and out of each of their foreheads sprouts a sharp black horn, some six or seven feet long. Commonly it dangles down like a turkey-cock's comb, but when a unicorn has a mind to fight or put it to any other use, what does he do but make it stand, and then it is as straight as an arrow."

Such sarcastic notes were rare. Most people believed implicitly in the unicorn; they gloried in its radiant power, its mystery, elusiveness and might. Perhaps to a people in many ways enchained (one historian has described life in the Middle Ages as "brutish and brief"), the unicorn, unfettered and wild, was the ultimate symbol of freedom.

Finally, as absolute proof of their existence, there were the spiraled horns of unicorns. The most famous doctors owned them and sold a pinch of the powdered horn for ten times its weight in gold. Even the somewhat skeptical Swiss scientist Konrad von Gesner, the "Father of Zoology," had to admit in 1551 that the unicorn "must be on earth, or else its horn would not exist."

MIGHTY MONOCEROS

In the collection of 13th-century Norse lore called *Konungs Skuggsja* (*The King's Mirror*), a father tells his son about "the wonders that are found in the Icelandic seas." Among them "there is a sort [of whale] called the narwhal, which may not be eaten for fear of disease, for men fall ill and die when they eat it. This whale is not large in size; it never grows larger than twenty ells [approximately 30 feet]. It is not at all savage but rather tries to avoid fishermen. It has teeth in its head, all small but one which projects from the front of the upper jaw. This tooth is handsome, well formed, and straight as an onion stem. It may grow to a length of seven ells [approximately 10 feet] and is as even and smooth as if shaped with a tool. It projects straight forward from the head when the whale is traveling; but sharp and straight though it is, it is of no service as a defensive weapon; for the whale is so fond and careful of its tusk that it allows nothing to come near it."

This is the earliest known description of a narwhal, and for many centuries it was also the most accurate, except for one blatant error, that narwhal meat is poisonous and that those who eat it may die. This belief has its origin in the narwhal's name, which is derived from the Old Norse words *nār*, "corpse" and *hvalr*, "whale." Some, among them the author of *The King's Mirror*, interpreted this to mean that those who eat its meat end up as corpses. The narwhal's "flesh is deadly poison," Thomas Pennant stated in his *Arctic Zoology* published in London in 1784, and the great geographer Gerhardus Mercator (1512–94) declared flatly that "among the fish [of Iceland] is included the Narwhal. Anyone who eats its flesh dies immediately."

Some scientists had a far more sinister interpretation for the narwhal's name —the whale that eats corpses. In the 1630s, while preparing his dissertation on "the horn of the unicorn," in which he exposed it as the tusk of the narwhal, the famous Danish zoologist and regius professor Ole Wurm, wrote to Thorlac Scalonius, bishop of Hole in Iceland, requesting information about the narwhal. The bishop sent him a painting of a narwhal and explained helpfully that Icelanders call the animal "narhual, signifying a whale which feeds on carcasses." Another 17th-century Danish professor, Thomas Bartholinus, wrote in his book *De Unicornu Observationes Novae* ("*New Observations About Unicorns*"), "In the vicinity of our island of Greenland and other northerly isles an enormous marine creature is a frequent denizen, popularly known as the narwhal because it feeds on dead bodies.''

As the unicorn legend lost some of its luster, the narwhal legend grew. In many accounts this shy whale of the Arctic becomes a demonic creature. John Laing, surgeon aboard the British whaling ship *Resolute*, sailed to Spitsbergen in 1806 and 1807 and returned with some typical whalers' tales: "The Sea Unicorn is another of the [bowhead] whale's enemies; and it is said that they never meet without engaging in combat. Its immense tusk . . . generally gives [the narwhal] a superiority over the [bowhead] whale." Not content with spearing 50-ton whales, the narwhal, Laing said, "swims with great swiftness and . . . has been known to dart its horn into the side of a ship."

Scientists took these tales and lovingly embellished them. In Georges Louis Leclerc, comte de Buffon's 44-volume *Histoire Naturelle*, published from 1749 to 1804, the narwhal is a bloodthirsty beast that "attacks the powerful, braves all dangers, seeks out carnage, attacks without provocation, has no equal in battle, and kills without need." With that as "scientific" basis, Jules Verne's perfervid imagination created a narwhal that is the ultimate monster — part gigantic narwhal, part supercharged electric eel. In *Twenty Thousand Leagues Under the Sea*, published in 1870, Verne begins mildly enough. "The ordinary narwhal," he explains, "is a kind of whale which grows to a length of sixty feet." Then the story picks up élan. This giant whale, Verne asserts, "is armed . . . with an ivory sword . . . as hard as steel" and with it, it can pierce ships "clean through as easily as a drill pierces a barrel." When the "narwhal" is finally sighted (really the submarine *Nautilus*), the hero of the story, Professor Pierre Aronax, exclaims, "It's obviously a gigantic narwhal and one that can produce electricity . . . the most terrible creature God ever invented."

The facts are slightly different. Narwhals are small whales; adult females reach 13 to 15 feet in length, males rarely exceed 17 feet. The ivory tusk is hollow and brittle. Narwhals are very shy; whalers rarely caught them. They eat primarily fishes and never corpses. Their flesh is excellent to eat and is a staple of the Polar Inuit of northwest Greenland. The ancient Norse named it "corpse whale" because of its peculiar mottled, splotched coloring, which reminded them of the grayish, blotched color of drowned sailors. The only one in England who seems to have been aware of this was the immensely well-informed Elizabethan poet Edmund Spenser, who wrote about the narwhal in *The Faerie Queene*:

Mighty Monoceros with immeasured tayles;
The dreadful Fish that hath deserved the name
Of Death, and like him looks in dreadful hew;

The narwhal is a very private whale, its realm remote, its life, from birth to

"The monoceros [narwhal] is a sea-monster . . . [with] a very long horn wherewith it can pierce and wreck vessels and destroy many men."

— OLAUS MAGNUS, Swedish archbishop, 1555

natural death, poorly known. Its close cousin, the talkative beluga, thrives in captivity, performs with apparent pleasure if rewarded, mates and bears young. The captive narwhal dies. An orphaned calf was airlifted in 1969 from the high Arctic to the New York Aquarium. In 1970, six narwhals were taken to the Vancouver Public Aquarium. All died after a few months in captivity. Bacterial and viral infections were said to have caused their deaths.

Narwhals usually live near ice, and it is among or near the arctic pack ice that they mate in mid-April. Only one man is known to have seen narwhals mating. A Polar Inuk spotted a pair in Melville Bay of northwest Greenland in the 1930s and told the Danish scientist Christian Vibe that "the whales copulated standing vertically in the water with their bellies turned to each other."

In summer narwhals swim into deep, ice-sheltered fiords and bays where, usually in mid-July after a 15-month gestation period, the well-padded, grayish calves are born. Female narwhals attain sexual maturity at the age of about five years. They have, at best, one calf every three years and in their lifetime probably not more than four or five. They guard these precious calves with infinite solicitude.

I watched them once from a helicopter hovering high above Koluktoo Bay, gray-spattered forms flecked with sunlight, small herds of females and their calves, each calf a miniature replica of its massive mother. They came from the deep, pale distorted forms that rose obliquely to the surface and suddenly became narwhals, the small, heart-shaped flukes of the calves rising and falling rapidly as they tried to keep pace with the powerful adults. They swam and breathed; far beneath I saw the tiny puffs of vapor rising. And then they stopped and lay quietly at the surface. Suddenly a gust of wind brought to them the clattering, metallic helicopter noise and instantly the mothers tried to shield their calves from the sensed but unseen danger. The calves dived first into the saving deep, the adults followed, diving steeply, and for an instant the sculptured magnificence of their flukes was outlined against the dark water. "In no living thing are the lines of beauty more exquisitely defined than in the crescentic borders of these flukes," wrote Herman Melville.

Calves are about five feet long at birth, weigh 180 pounds, and are wrapped in a one-inch-thick layer of insulating blubber, which protects them from the sapping cold of the arctic sea. For about two years mother and calf are inseparable. She feeds it frequently with fat-rich milk, talks to it in little squeals and grunts, and occasionally plays with it. The Canadian biologist Holly Cleator watched a narwhal mother and her young from a cliff above Koluktoo Bay. The mother made a shallow dive and surfaced a moment later beneath her calf. It rolled and slipped over her round, rubbery head. She dived, nudged it again, and this time the calf slithered across her broad back, flukes flapping, a happy, gentle game of bump and glide.

Calves are a uniform slate gray. In immatures the belly becomes at first pale

*The setting sun sets fog and clouds aglow
above Koluktoo Bay, Baffin Island, where
hundreds of narwhals spend the summer.*

Tusks clash as male narwhals vie for dominance. Flip Nicklin

gray, then gleaming white and satin-smooth to the touch. The adult, said Melville, "has a very picturesque leopard-like look, being of milk-white ground color, dotted with round and oblong spots of black." With advancing age, even these black blotches begin to pale.

While I lived with the Polar Inuit of northwest Greenland, they harpooned and killed an ancient male. His tusk was a massive, broken stump, his skin pure white with a few faint grayish spots upon his back and sides. The smoothness of his skin was marred by many scars. Some, on the back, were probably old gunshot wounds; others, on the head and neck, were perhaps inflicted by the tusks of rival males. The indented scars were packed with parasites known as narwhal lice (*Cyamus monodontis*). They are really highly specialized little crustaceans that cling to their sleek and fast-swimming host with needle-sharp, sickle-shaped legs. Despite his age, his old wounds and the mass of parasites, the male was in superb condition. He weighed about 3,600 pounds, close to the 4,000-pound maximum known for narwhals, and he was swathed in blubber slightly more than four inches thick.

Determining a whale's age is an ancient art. Aristotle knew more than 2,000 years ago that dolphins live for "twenty-five, and some for thirty years" and explained that "fishermen nick their tails sometimes and set them adrift again, and by this expedient their ages are ascertained." In narwhals the tusk is sectioned and its growth layers, similar to the annual rings in trees, tell scientists the animal's age. Those that have been cut up for age studies have revealed that narwhals may live for up to thirty years.

The Comte de Buffon believed, as did many others, that the tusked narwhal skewers fish and eats them *en brochette*. Narwhals are efficient hunters, but they probably never use their tusks. They usually hunt alone. They dive deep, to a thousand feet and more, plane above the ocean floor, snap up silt-gray Greenland halibut, and crush spiny, big-headed sculpins with their hard-edged, toothless jaws. They swim through shoals of dancing shrimp and swallow mouthfuls of the crusty crustaceans, rich in fat and protein. Sometimes they hunt in efficient groups, herding schools of polar cod, the immensely abundant, silvery-sided fish of the Far North that is the narwhal's favorite prey.

I watched the hunting whales one night in mid-August from the coast of Inglefield Bay in northwest Greenland. The tides were the highest of the year and fish and whales came close to shore. Clouds of screaming kittiwakes hovered above the water, dived and rose with fish. The narwhals hunted in teams just beneath the surface, five to ten whales driving the massed fish towards one another. At such hunts the whales gorge themselves; each narwhal may eat 200 pounds of fish. In 1924, the explorer-writer Peter Freuchen killed a narwhal in Baffin Island's Eclipse Sound, "its stomach so stuffed with small tom-cod [polar cod], that it could hold no more. Nevertheless, mouth, throat, even the corners of the jaws were stuffed; I have never seen an animal so replete."

Icelanders call it "narhual, signifying a whale which feeds on carcasses, because hual means a whale, and nar, a dead body."

— THORLAC SCALONIUS, Icelandic bishop, ca 1630

The tusk is "used mainly to deliver frontal blows . . . when the Narwhal defends the young and the females from Arctic sharks."

— A.G. TOMILIN, Russian scientist, 1967

Overleaf: *Once threatened with extinction, the polar bear population has increased thanks to government protection and management.*

What sets the narwhal apart is not its ambiguous and slightly sinister name, its strange color, or its remote and icy home, but the ivory tusk of the male, which looks like a cross between a corkscrew and a jousting lance. Ever since it became known, humans have expended an extraordinary amount of ingenuity and fantasy to explain why the narwhal should have a tusk and what he does with it, with conjectures ranging from such wild pursuits as piercing ships or bowhead whales, to such mild pursuits as poking up seaweed.

All narwhals have two teeth in their upper jaw and no others. In females these teeth are ten-inch-long, finger-thick ivory rods, which normally remain hidden in the alveoli, the tooth sockets within the jaw. In about three percent of all females, the left tooth erupts and becomes a spiraled tusk, usually slim and rarely longer than four feet. There is one amazing exception. The skull of a female narwhal with twin tusks, both nearly seven feet long, was given to a museum in Hamburg, Germany, in 1684 by a whaling captain who had killed the pregnant animal near Spitsbergen.

In the male, the right tooth normally remains embedded. When the male calf is about a year old, its left tooth continues to grow, pierces the upper lip and spirals onward, counterclockwise, until, in the fully grown male the tusk reaches a maximum length of about ten feet, and a maximum basal girth of eight or nine inches. The tusk is round, evenly tapered, and hollow for most of its length, and the cavity is filled with dental pulp. About one foot of the tusk is "screwed" into the narwhal's large, flat, asymmetrical skull. The tips of most tusks are shining white and usually smoothly polished; the grooves are densely packed with greenish algae.

About one male in 500 has two tusks, the left one usually longer and stronger. Both tusks spiral in the same direction, from right to left. Few people in the Arctic ever see a double-tusked narwhal; the surgeon John Laing aboard the whaler *Resolute* saw two in a single day. On June 10, 1806, near Spitsbergen "several of the sea-unicorns [were] at no great distance from the ship. I noticed two . . . had double horns of a considerable size." Its tusk is now the narwhal's curse. Tusked males are intensively pursued and the rare twin-tusked whales are doubly cursed. In 1978, a bidentate narwhal skull sold for $5,000 in Pond Inlet.

At least a third of all narwhal tusks are broken, most near the tip, some in the middle. Of a few only a jagged stump remains. The exposed dental tissue is usually inflamed and has a nasty, putrid smell. The poor whale, one imagines, suffers a massive toothache. The open end of the hollow tusk is often plugged with sediment or pebbles. Inuit say the whale, frantic with pain, rams its broken tusk into the ocean floor to fill the cavity.

The Danish scientist Morton P. Porsild, who examined hundreds of narwhal tusks in Greenland, wrote in 1922 that "the strangest feature is, however, that not seldom a point of another, smaller tusk is found thrust into the cavity and then broken off, a real 'tooth-filling'." The Inuit told Porsild "wonderful

tales about it. They say an old male with a broken tusk entices a young one to thrust its tusk into the cavity, whereupon by a jerk, it breaks the tusk of the younger narwhal."

The French author Isaac de la Peyrère tells in his *Relation de Groënland* that in 1640 the king of Denmark "wishing to make a present of a piece of [his] horn" ordered it cut, "came to a cavity, and was astonished to find within a small horn, of the same shape and composition as the large one . . . the little horn extending a foot in length." While some scientists now think that these tusks-within-tusks are the result of head-on jousting, others have a more prosaic explanation; it is, they say, a dentine plug created by the healing tusk.

For centuries, whalers, explorers and scientists have imagined ever more ingenious uses for the narwhal's tusk. "He uses this horn to get at the sea-grass, which is its proper food," wrote the Moravian missionary David Crantz in 1768, and added that the narwhal "also bores a hole in the ice with it when he wants fresh air." Peter Freuchen said the tusk was used to poke up bottom-dwelling flatfish. The Russian scientist A.G. Tomilin thought the tusk was "mainly used to deliver frontal blows . . . when the Narwhal defends the young and the females from Arctic sharks." Melville, amused by all the theories, opined in *Moby Dick* that the tusk might serve the narwhal as a letter opener. That astute observer, the whaler-scientist William Scoresby, said early in the 19th century that the tusk was merely an ornament of the male, a secondary sexual characteristic, like a cock's comb, a man's beard, or a lion's mane.

Modern theories are much fancier than the simple ice auger and fish spear ideas of the past. It has been proposed that the white-polished tusk tip acts as a lure attracting phototropic prey and that the tusk cleaves water and reduces drag. Some dental specialists believe that the tusk is a cooling mechanism with which the blubber-insulated narwhal "eliminates excess body heat generated by spurts of abnormal physical activity." Perhaps the most intriguing notion has been advanced by Canadian bio-acoustician Peter Beamish, who believes the males may use their tusks for "acoustic jousting," focusing high-intensity sounds through the hollow tusk at the opponent's sensitive ear. In such duels the whale with the longer tusk wins, because he is the first to deafen his rival.

Since only males have tusks, it is surprising how rarely it was assumed that rival males might use the tusks like rapiers to duel for the favor of the tuskless females. "They seem to fight with them," said the British naturalist Robert Brown in 1868, and Pond Inlet Inuit told the Canadian geologist and explorer A.P. Low in 1903 that narwhals use their tusks "for domestic battle." As old males are often deeply scarred, it seemed a fair assumption that these might be battle scars. Then, in August of 1957, the Inuk George Moto found a beached narwhal near Candle, Alaska, and embedded in its left upper jaw was the broken point of another narwhal's tusk. Now extensive observations by the Canadian scientists Helen Silverman and M.J. Dunbar, and John and Deborah

The narwhal's tusk "is of no service as a defensive weapon; for the whale is so fond and careful of its tusk that it allows nothing to come near it."

— *The King's Mirror*, author unknown, 13th-century Iceland

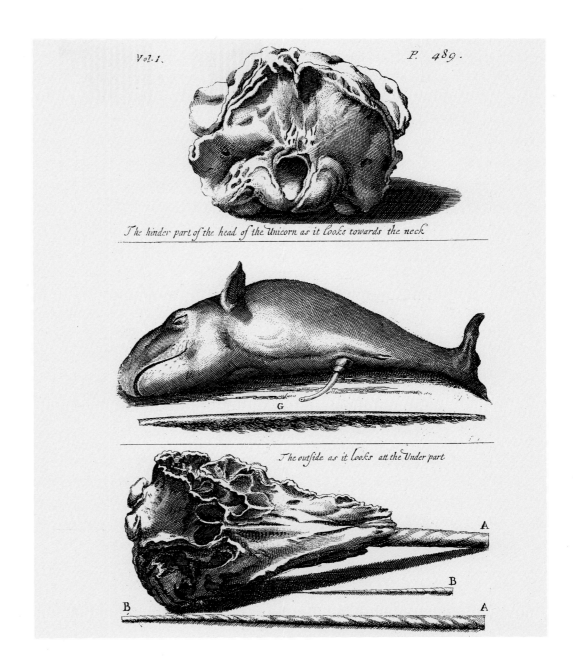

Ford have confirmed that the tusk is indeed used for jousting.

Narwhal males cross their tusks like swords in contests above or below the water, and strike their tusks together with an oddly wooden, clacking sound. Young narwhal males, like young males of many species, including humans, playfight; they spar a lot but rarely spear each other. Silverman and Dunbar have noted that, as males reach sexual maturity at eight or nine years of age, tusk girth and length increase rapidly. The tusk becomes a badge of supremacy; the longer the tusk, the greater the power and prestige of the male. Fights establish dominance and hierarchical standing, ritual jousting maintains it, and the most powerful males with the longest tusks mate with the most females. The tusk is the measure of the male and, as in the unicorn, it is the symbol of his potency and power.

THE MAGIC HORN

In 1596, Queen Elizabeth I of England sent Sir Henry Winton to France as her ambassador. Shortly after his arrival at the court of King Henry IV, Sir Henry became violently ill. It was assumed he had been poisoned, a not unreasonable assumption because poisoning for private or political reasons was fairly common in England and France, although in neither country was it carried out with the expertise and finesse achieved in Renaissance Italy. According to a contemporary account, the sick ambassador ". . . was physicked with Confectio Alcarmas, which was composed of unicorn's horn, musk, amber, gold and pearls, and with pidgeons applied to his side and all other means that art could devise, sufficient to expell the strongest poison . . ."

To be poisoned was a major professional hazard for medieval and Renaissance princes and potentates. It was a favorite means employed by restive nobles and disgruntled subjects to rid themselves of unloved rulers. However, not only subjects used poison; kings and queens could be particularly dangerous. Marie de'Medici (1573–1642), queen of France, employed a personal poisoner, an unctuous Florentine with blotchy hands and a cold serpent's smile. The Medicis were a brilliant but lethal family. It was said that Marie's father, Francis I, Grand-duke of Tuscany, was poisoned by his brother, the Cardinal Ferdinand, and her mother died 15 hours later.

Arsenic was probably the favorite poison. It was cheap, deadly and readily available. Taken internally it produced violent cramps, vomiting and death due to heart or kidney failure. Poisoners occasionally impregnated the clothing of their intended victims with poison; slowly absorbed through the skin, it brought on slow death. The 14th-century King John of Castile died, according to reports, after wearing poison-soaked boots; England's King Henry VI (1421–71) reputedly succumbed to poisoned gloves; and that famous patron of the arts and owner of several unicorn horns, Pope Clement VII (1475–1534)— also a Medici—died after inhaling smoke from an ingeniously poisoned processional torch.

Aconitine, often called "the queen mother of all poisons," was obtained from the rootstocks of the cowl-shaped, deep-blue monkshood plant, or from the yellow wolfsbane (so named because it was believed this plant could also repel werewolves). Within moments of ingestion, aconitine produced a freezing

Above: *A pod of narwhal near ice in Lancaster Sound.*

Opposite: *Male narwhals thrust and parry. Tusk length and the power of the male determine his social standing.* Flip Nicklin

sensation that crept outward from the core of the body. Eventually paralysis stopped the victim's heart. Shakespeare in *King Henry IV* speaks of the "venom of suggestion" that works "as strong as aconitum." Hemlock, a common marsh plant, brought slow suffocation. A pinch of henbane produced mad exhilaration followed by violent cramps and sudden death.

Apart from the royal practitioners and their helpers, there were highly skilled professionals, such as the Milanese poisoner Aqua Toffana of whom the British author Odell Shepard writes that "she is said to have disposed of more than six hundred persons during her half-century of practice, before she was publicly strangled at the age of seventy." In 17th-century Paris some of the ladies who sold love potions also dealt, on the sly, in small envelopes filled with poison, popularly known as "inheritance powders."

Several substances were believed to be able to detect poison: bezoar-stone, snake's tongue, griffin's claw, and the strange and giant coco-de-mer. Each fruit of this tall fan palm, which grows on the Seychelle Islands in the Indian Ocean, can weigh up to 100 pounds. It was reportedly so efficacious in combating poison, the famous English botanist William J. Hooker noted in 1827 that "some kings [in fear of death by poison] have given a loaded ship for a single nut."

All these substances, however, were of small importance, oddities used in an emergency. The one antidote rulers craved, the alexipharmic *sans pareil* for more than 4,000 years, was the horn of the unicorn. "Genuine unicorn [horn] is good against all poison," declared the Swiss scientist and physician Konrad von Gesner in 1551. "Experience proves that anyone having taken poison . . . recovered good health on immediately taking a little unicorn horn."

As a result of this deeply held conviction, all those in fear of poison purchased unicorn horns or fragments thereof and looked upon them as an essential though costly protection. "Is there any Prince, Duke, or King in the world," the German scholar J.F. Hubrigk demanded in 1660, "who has not either seen or possessed, and regarded as among the most precious of his possessions, a unicorn's horn?" It was used in palaces and refectories, and no wise traveler left home without it. In 1591, the English explorer Thomas Cavendish stopped at a town in Brazil and "all our men . . . fell sick by eating of a kind of sweet pleasant fruit that was poison and had it not been for a gentleman called Enefrio de Say . . . who had a piece of Unicornes horn we had all died."

Belief in the antidotal properties of unicorn horn came from the East, especially India, where the original unicorn was probably the rhinoceros. But in the West and large parts of the East, the much more distinctive, elegant and impressive narwhal tusk became the "unicorn horn," its true nature proclaimed by the unique spiral, its "cochleary turnings," as the English physician Sir Thomas Browne (1605–82) put it. It was this horn that princes coveted and that was worth ten times its weight in gold.

The Countess of Bath bequeathed to her daughter Dame Elizabeth Kytson "her caskanet of pearls, with the flower of diamonds . . . and her unicorns [horn]."

— COUNTESS OF BATH, 1561

A fierce narwhal-tusked unicorn in the German edition of Albertus Magnus' famous bestiary, published in Frankfurt in 1545.

The sinister Tomas de Torquemada (1420–98), who headed Spain's grim Inquisition, never sat at table without having all his food and drink tested with his unicorn horn. The Holy Roman Emperor Charles V (1500–58) settled what in today's terms would be a multi-million-dollar debt with the Margrave of Bayreuth by giving him two unicorn horns. The city of Dresden in Germany paid 75,000 thalers for its unicorn horn. Occasionally a bit of powder was filed from this horn to be used as medicine, and a Dresden city regulation required two persons of princely rank to be present when this operation was performed. The first wife of Robert Dudley, Earl of Leicester and favorite of Queen Elizabeth I, died abruptly and conveniently, presumably of poison. In 1576, fearing that he, in turn, might be poisoned, he demanded from the Warden and Fellows of New College, Oxford, the unicorn horn in their possession. They compromised by sawing off the tip and sending it to Leicester. The truncated horn is still in the muniment room of New College.

Since they were so immensely valuable, unicorn horns made ideal gifts between rulers, expressing by their value and the nature of their use a nice mixture of munificence, concern and, perhaps, warning. Considering the reputation of Catherine de'Medici, it was most thoughtful of her uncle, Pope Clement VII (the one who succumbed to a poisoned torch), to present her father-in-law King Francis I with a beautifully mounted unicorn horn when she married the dauphin of France in 1533. The most lavish gift of all came from the world's wealthiest ruler; the Sultan of Turkey sent 12 unicorn horns to His Most Catholic Majesty King Philip II of Spain (1527–98).

As food was brought to the royal table, a tester touched viands and wines with the unicorn horn. If they contained poison, the unicorn horn would make them "froth darkly" and bubble. Unicorn horn, according to a near-universal

*The magnificent northwest Greenland coast
mirrored in the glassy waters of a bay.*

Walrus ivory from arctic Russia and Siberia traveled along ancient trade routes to Central Asia, China and the Middle East.

belief, "exuded" in the presence of poison; it began to gleam and drip with sweaty beads. Therefore horns, usually set into solid-gold holders that were often encrusted with jewels, stood on many royal tables to provide an early poison warning. Since would-be-poisoners believed all this and hence desisted, the unicorn horns, no doubt, saved many lives. Inevitably, there were slips. In 1585, the Duke of Anjou died suddenly after his valet had "forgotten" to test his wine with a unicorn horn. The poison, it was rumored, had been administered by the duke's mother, the lovely but lethal Catherine de'Medici.

Since unicorns and unicorn horns were so closely associated with royalty and power, it is not surprising that two scepters, the ultimate symbol of imperial power, and one throne were made of unicorn horns. In addition to the scepter of Austria's Habsburgs, Russia's imperial scepter has as its shaft a fairly slender unicorn horn. This scepter was used for the first time on June 10, 1584, at the coronation of Tsar Feodor I. The English ambassador, Jerome Horsey, attended the magnificent ceremony and reported that the tsar wore his "chiefe imperiall Crowne upon his head" and "his staffe imperiall in his right hand of an unicornes horne of three foot and a halfe in length beset with rich stones, bought of Merchants of Augsburge [Germany] by the old Emperour [Ivan IV, the Terrible] in An. 1581, and cost him 7000 Markes sterling."

Because most narwhal tusks came from Greenland, then Danish-owned, the kings of Denmark had the largest collection of these tusks. They believed as passionately and totally as everyone else that these were, in fact, unicorn horns. From the finest of these horns, a throne was built and on June 7, 1671, King Christian V became the first Danish monarch to be crowned seated upon the Unicorn Throne, which became instantly famous as one of the wonders of Europe. Comparing it to Solomon's throne, which was made of ivory and gold, the officiating bishop declaimed that "your Majesty is also sitting on a costly throne which in the glory of its material . . . is like unto Solomon's throne, and the like thereof cannot be found in any kingdom."

To medieval and Renaissance man, unicorn horn was the all-healing magic medicine, the panacea of the ages. It could not only warn of poison and heal a poisoned person, but it could also cure all human ills. In exceptional circumstances it was widely bruited, it could even raise the dead. It was the sine qua non of every important physician and pharmacist. "This horn is useful and beneficial against epilepsy," wrote Konrad von Gesner in 1551. "[It will cure] pestilent fever, rabies, proliferation and infection of vermin, and [destroy] the worms within the body from which children faint."

A 17th-century doctor's poster in London promised that unicorn horn would heal, among other things, scurvy, ulcers, dropsy, gout, coughs, consumption, fainting fits, the "Kings Evil" [scrofula], rickets in children, melancholy, the "Green Sickness" [chlorosis], and obstructions. In addition, the poster promised that a drink made with unicorn horn would fortify "the noble parts" and

"Physicians are frequently compelled to prescribe unicorn [horn] . . . because [patients] demand such remedies."

— AMBROISE PARÉ, surgeon to four kings of France, 1510–90

Denmark's famous Unicorn Throne was built of narwhal tusks and walrus ivory. In 1671, King Christian V became the first Danish monarch to be crowned on this unique throne. The Royal Danish Collections, Rosenborg Palace

A calf stays with its mother for about two years. She talks to it in little squeals and grunts. Animals Animals © Doug Allan

Among male narwhals tusk length determines social standing. Flip Nicklin

preserve "Vigour, Youth and a good Complexion to Old Age." On top of all its other virtues, the unicorn horn was a renowned aphrodisiac. A 17th-century account promises that it will "overcome feminine modesty and resistance, and [also] cure corns, heartburn, and sore eyes . . ." Truly a medicine for all ailments and occasions, it made barren women abundantly fertile, impotent men magnificently potent, and it also cured "the pox," venereal disease.

The unicorn became the emblem of the pharmacist. When the Apothecaries' Society of London was founded in 1617, two unicorns were chosen as supporters of its arms. Families with unicorns in their escutcheons, such as the well-known Baltic-German family von Krüdener, may once have dealt in medicine. To this day in Germany many pharmacies carry the name *die Einhornapotheke*, "the unicorn pharmacy." In case of illness, "unicorn powder" was scraped from the horn and mixed with water or wine. The patient paid plenty and then drank this potion. It did, of course, not always work. When Martin Luther, then 62, was gravely ill in Eisleben, he was given "doses of ground unicorn horn in wine . . . but died nevertheless in the morning of February 18, 1546."

> "I saw among the Venetians [a compound made] of lime and soap or other which things [and sold as] unicorn's horn."
>
> — RICHARD HAKLUYT, English geographer, 1589

A 17th-century London doctor's poster praises the powers of unicorn horn. Bodleian Library (Wood 534 III b)

"It was a common procedure [in medieval time] to dip the [unicorn horn] into a well or spring to purify the water."

— JOHN TYLER BONNER, professor, Princeton University, 1951

Such failures were not widely reported. Faith in the marvelous, saving horn was near-universal, prices were fabulous, and fraud was frequent. The most common substitutes for powdered unicorn horn were crushed pig bones, whale bones, fossils, limestone, and various types of clay, usually mixed with soap.

To make fraudulent unicorn powder was, of course, simple. To make a saleable ersatz horn or even pieces thereof, so perfect that some princely schnook would shell out for it, was much more complicated because of the true unicorn's unique and telltale spiral shape. However, ingenious frauds were made. The Hamburg Museum of Arts and Crafts owns two "unicorn" beakers. One is "genuine"; it is made of a narwhal tusk. The other is a brilliant imitation, the essential spirals cut into walrus ivory by a superbly skilled forger.

The 16th-century French traveler André Thevet visited one center for making imitation unicorn horns — an island in the Red Sea. There clever and highly trained artisans steamed elephant and walrus tusks for ten to twenty hours, or boiled them for six hours in a decoction of mandrake, thinned and elongated the softened tusks, gave them the distinctive torque of narwhal tusks and sold them at a fabulous profit in Europe, the Middle East and Asia as "genuine unicorn horns."

Unicorn horn was, for at least 600 years, one of the most valuable substances in Europe. Rulers paid fortunes for their horns. There was a widespread and immensely lucrative trade in them. Yet somehow it doesn't seem to have bothered anyone, that in all this time not a single unicorn was ever seen. There were, of course, rumors and romances and wonderful tales brought back by travelers, but not one unicorn, alive or dead, was ever shown at court or in the market. Only the horns existed, those lovely spiraled tusks, and medieval man and even questing Renaissance man was willing to accept both the animal and its magic horn on faith alone.

There were, in truth, a few doubters and dissenters, as early as the 16th and 17th centuries. The immensely learned Sir Thomas Browne remarked "with what security a man may rely on [unicorn horn], the mistress of fools [death] hath already instructed us." The great Ambroise Paré (1510–90), physician to four kings of France (and to Catherine de'Medici) thought unicorn horn had little or no medicinal value but noted realistically: "Physicians are frequently compelled to prescribe unicorn . . . because [patients] demand such remedies. For if it happened that a patient who had made such a request were to die without receiving what he wanted, the family would expel such physicians and disparage them in gossip as 'quite out of touch.'" So Paré prescribed unicorn horn, charged the equivalent of $1,200 for a smidgen, smiled and wrote in his diary: "C'est que le monde veult estre trompé" — "What the world wants is to be cheated." This was true and hence no one listened when in 1569 the Flemish historian Goropius of Antwerp said, "I sometimes suspect that this is the horn of some fish."

INUIT AND *TUGALIK*

On July 13, 1971, a sudden storm broke up the ice and drove it out of Inglefield Bay in northwest Greenland, the central hunting region of the Polar Inuit and summer home to some 4,000 narwhals. Here, every July since time immemorial, narwhals have come and the world's northernmost people have hunted them. For weeks the people at our camp at Inerssussat had thought *kilaluga* ("narwhal"), talked *kilaluga*, dreamt *kilaluga*. They were totally immersed in the wish-thought world of the hunter. They sat on a bluff near camp and scanned the great bay with intense concentration and powerful binoculars until someone sang out, "*Kilaluga-hoi!*" — the narwhals are coming.

The men raced to the beach, launched their sleek sealskin-covered kayaks — the most beautiful and efficient hunting boats ever designed — and paddled stealthily and swiftly across the wind-rippled sea into the assumed path of the approaching whales. On the bluff the women clustered, tense with anticipation and excitement. The early summer seal hunt had been poor, supplies were dwindling, and for the past two weeks we had lived primarily on sculpin, bony little fish that we caught through tidal ice cracks near shore.

The men fanned out across part of the bay and then were totally still. Their white-painted kayaks looked like ice, and many lay near ice floes and small bergs to avoid detection by the wary whales. The narwhals, half a dozen pods with from ten to twenty animals in each, swam leisurely towards the faraway head of the bay, a favorite summer feeding area. Blunt, bulging heads broke the surface, little puffs of vapor rose from blowholes, and smooth dark backs slid through the sea. The hunters were in place and waiting, silent, motionless. "Narwhals are extremely difficult to hunt because of their incredibly sharp hearing," said the Canadian author Doug Wilkinson, who spent a year with the Pond Inlet Inuit and hunted with them in the early 1950s. "The sound of a drop of water on the deck of the kayak is enough to send them streaking for the depth."

Only one hunter had a chance. As a group of whales passed close to Jes Qujaukitsoq, he slipped his kayak smoothly into their wake and then paddled with all his strength. That is the narwhal's weakest spot; when the kayak is directly behind the whale he cannot see it and, perhaps because of the turbulence created by his wake, often does not hear it. Jes paddled flat out to catch

Above: *The tusks of these dueling narwhal males clash with an odd, wooden clacking noise. On rare occasions, a male thrusts his tusk into his opponent's head or side.* Flip Nicklin

Opposite: *Masautsiaq, a famous narwhal hunter, paddles out into Inglefield Bay.*

up with the whales. Upon the bluff the women were in a frenzy of excitement, urging on the tiny figure in the distance like rooters at a football game. But this was not sport, it was food and life, endurance and skill, and the age-old thrill of the hunt.

When Jes was close behind the whale, he grabbed his heavy, ivory-tipped harpoon, threw it with one smooth, immensely powerful motion and a second later the women screamed in jubilation, "*Avatak! Avatak!*" The harpoon had struck and the *avatak*, the sealskin float, danced upon the water; the stricken whale was doomed. The other kayaks converged upon the whale. The instant it surfaced, the closest man threw a harpoon, another a third, and soon after they killed the whale with lances. They lashed *avataks* to the carcass to keep it afloat, tied their kayaks in tandem and hauled the heavy, inert load to camp. Jes alone was free, skimming along in front with easy flicks of his paddle. As they neared shore, he cried in triumph to the women and children assembled on the beach: "We bring the *kilaluga*! We bring *tugalik* ['the tusked male whale']!" And then the hordes arrived. Nearly every wage-employed Inuk from the nearby village of Qaanaaq—and his family—came running to claim a share of the whale.

Until recently the dead whale was divided according to an ancient custom full of fairness, dignity and wisdom. The man who threw the first harpoon received the head and tusk, a large piece of the finest *muktuk* (the vitamin-rich narwhal skin that tastes like hazelnuts) and a choice cut of meat. The second harpoon thrower took smaller pieces, and thus every hunter received a share in proportion to his contribution to the hunt, its size fixed by tradition. However, not only the participating hunters shared. Anyone could come to the beach and claim a portion of the whale simply by touching it. In this way, some of the old or disabled obtained their food. They took it not as charity but by ancient right, a system devised by a proud and generous people.

This was the tradition of the hunters, but with the advent of a parallel wage economy, the system went awry. As soon as the hunters beached the whale, the well-paid citizens of Qaanaaq streamed to the shore and helped themselves to *muktuk* and to meat. Sharing food is an Inuk custom. But wages were never shared. That is a European custom. And thus Inerssussat, one of the best hunting spots in the region, was slowly being abandoned. The hunters moved away from the village, to faraway camps inhabited only by other hunters and their families, where sharing remained mutual.

In the 13th century, when the climate became much colder and the Little Ice Age began, Inuit left the farthest north or died out. All except the Polar Inuit of the immensely game-rich Thule region. For about 500 years, until they were "discovered" by the British explorer John Ross, the 200-odd Polar Inuit lived in total isolation. During their long isolation, they lost the art of kayak making (they remembered kayaks as mythical craft), but were immensely skillful

If you "meet with any Esquemaux you are to treat them Civily . . . and encourage them to Trade . . . Unicorns Horns . . ."

— HUDSON'S BAY COMPANY instructions to captains, 1798

at hunting narwhals among the ice. The Polar Inuit, said Ross in 1818, "eat all kinds of animal food; but the seal and the sea unicorn are preferred . . . The sea unicorn is taken by a harpoon . . . and as he frequents the chasms and pools in the ice, he falls an easy prey to the natives."

In a land where even a small piece of driftwood was rare and precious, narwhal tusks took the place of wood. With the simplest of tools and great skill and ingenuity, the Inuit made sled runners from the tusks, which they also used as tent poles. Their lances, noted the American explorer Elisha Kent Kane in 1854, were "quite a formidable weapon. The staff was the horn of a narwhal." Other Inuit groups used narwhal tusks for similar objects. Lieutenant Edward Chappell of Britain's Royal Navy stopped in 1814 at the Savage Islands in Hudson Strait, where the natives showed him their arrows "headed with sea-unicorn's horn." When the famous American anthropologist Franz Boas visited the people of Canada's northern Foxe Basin in 1884, he found that "the narwhal's horn was the favorite material [for harpoons], a single horn being sufficient to make a whole shaft." And my old friend Masautsiaq, a Polar Inuk with whom I lived for many months, recalled that in his youth in the early 1920s, a few old men still used *ipu* handles made of narwhal tusks. The *ipu*, the long-handled net used to catch dovekies, small fat seabirds, another essential Polar Inuit food, is still used, but now the handles are made of bamboo.

To the Polar Inuit the narwhals were vital. The Danish scientist Christian Vibe lived among them for more than a year and wrote in 1940, "The whole existence of the Polar Eskimos depends on the catch of this animal, since they get all their necessaries of life from it." The whales were just as important to the people when I went to live with them in 1971. From Inerssussat, where cultures were in collision, I moved to Kangerdlugssuaq, a remote camp near the head of Inglefield Bay where only hunting families lived.

A small river raced down from *sermerssuaq*, "the giant glacier," as Polar Inuit call the two-mile-thick ice cap of Greenland. Near it stood our tents, an ancient sod house, and tent rings and rock caches of great antiquity, for here Inuit had hunted narwhals for hundreds, perhaps thousands, of years. Beyond our camp in the bay lay a small island with a history, Qingmiunegarfiq, "the place where one leaves dogs" (in summer). Inuit think of themselves as the primal people to whom the very earth herself gave birth. For whites they postulate a less flattering ancestry; they are descended from an Inuk girl who went to Qingmiunegarfiq and mated there with one of the dogs. Since the offspring from this unfortunate union were a general embarrassment, they were put into a boat, drifted far to the south and became the ancestors of all whites, and that accounts for their pushiness, their restlessness, and for their poor manners.

In narwhal hunting, Canadian Inuit have chosen the modern way. They hunt the whales in summer with high-powered boats and shoot them with high-powered rifles. The hunt is fast, exciting, very expensive, and often extremely

Narwhals upon the beach at Koluktoo Bay on Baffin Island.

Cut into strips, narwhal meat dries on racks near camp, an important food for the winter months.

Where Inuit cut up narwhals, Greenland sharks are apt to come close to shore, attracted by the smell of blood.

Narwhal sinew is the best thread for sewing fur clothing and skin boots.

wasteful since whales are shot first and then, if possible, harpooned. Many sink and are lost or, severely wounded, escape and die later. The sea mammal specialists Kerry Finley and Garry Miller made a detailed study of the 1979 narwhal hunt near Pond Inlet and reported to the International Whaling Commission that "the commercial value of the narwhal tusk is a major incentive for the killing of a narwhal" and that "the introduction of modern technology has contributed to wasteful and inefficient hunting." They estimated that at least 50 percent of all whales killed are lost; they sink before they can be harpooned and retrieved.

In other studies, the loss figure is much higher; for every whale killed and retrieved, three or four are killed and lost. The permissible narwhal kill in the Canadian Arctic is regulated by a community quota system. Altogether, 542 whales may be taken, but this does not include losses. The total annual kill is

Ancient skills are passed from generation to generation. Sewing the sealskin cover onto the kayak frame requires experience. Old women usually sew the most difficult seams.

Polar Inuit gaff dead Greenland halibut which have drifted up into a lead. The flatfish will be fed to their sled dogs. The Greenland halibut is also a major food fish of narwhals.

at least twice that figure and may be as high as 1,500 or 2,000 animals. The older Inuit worry about the waste. One Pond Inlet hunter, Appaq, told Finley: "As Inuit who wish to have meat available in the future, we must carefully consider our hunting. As men, we must undertake to tell our children about the hunt so that they will be better able to follow us . . . We must tell our children not to waste meat in the hunt."

The Polar Inuit have opted for the old ways that demand great skill and endurance but are efficient and avoid waste. Narwhals may only be hunted with kayaks, and they must be harpooned before they are killed with lances or with guns. Few animals are ever lost and, as before, the whales provide the people with many "of the necessaries of life. . . ."

At Kangerdlugsuaq our existence flowed in the ancient, timeless rhythm of the hunter's life. Brief bursts of utmost exertion were followed by long periods

The sleek, fast kayak is perhaps the most beautiful and efficient hunting craft ever designed by man.

Inuit hunt the narwhal for its meat, its vitamin-rich skin and the valuable ivory tusks of the males. Janet Foster/Masterfile

of rest and leisurely work. Ululik Duneq with whom I lived, a thickset man in his late fifties, had come to camp with two three-quarter-inch planks. Using a knife, saw and plane, he transformed them gradually into a beautifully made kayak skeleton. His wife, Aqatanguak, helped by other women in camp, sewed the kayak's sealskin cover. The children watched, or helped, or played far into the luminous night. Ours was a simple life, relaxed, quiet, harmonious. But whatever we did, someone always scanned the bay, and when he or she cried, "*Kilaluga-hoi!*" all else was dropped and the ancient drama of the hunt began, sometimes successful, often not.

When the hunters returned in triumph with a whale, everyone in camp helped to heave the heavy carcass ashore, and then we stood quietly and admired it, but no one touched it. That, by ancient tradition, is the prerogative

A woman cleans narwhal sinew that will be used as an extremely strong thread.

of the man who first harpooned the whale. He cut a thin strip of *muktuk* from the leading edge of the fluke. By this symbolic gesture, he invited us to share. We knelt around the whale and ate, first *muktuk*, then chunks of raw, maroon-colored meat with snippets of creamy-white, high-energy blubber.

After this common meal, the whale was divided according to ancient custom. Each hunter took the exact portion to which he was entitled. An old couple touched the whale, then took their share of meat, fat and *muktuk*. In all the weeks I lived at the camp I never heard an argument.

About half of the meat and some of the fat is cached as food for the sled dogs. When working in winter (and winters are long in the Thule region; July is the only month of the year with an average temperature above the freezing point), they receive about a pound of meat and a quarter pound of fat each day.

Feeding sled dogs at a hunting camp.

Kayaks upon their racks near camp; icebergs gleam against the black sky of an approaching storm.

*Polar Inuit hunters return to shore with the
narwhal they have killed.*

The region's 1,200 sled dogs consume 400,000 pounds of meat and 100,000 pounds of fat per year.

The rest of the meat is cut into strips and dried on racks and rocks near camp. Leathery but protein-rich, *nipku*, narwhal jerky (". . . dried unicorn's flesh, which appeared to have been parched," said Ross in 1818) is an important winter food. It is sliced thinly and eaten with whale or seal oil. A few great chunks of meat, fat and skin, especially entire tails of whales, are stored in special blubber-lined caches where they slowly age for a year or more and become *iterssoraq*, "fermented meat." Its skin is bright green, the blubber olive green, the meat black and greenishly marbled, and the taste of the different parts ranges roughly from Brie, to Roquefort, to strong Stilton, to pungent old Gorgonzola, a spicy change from our usually bland diet of raw or boiled meat and blubber.

Not all the skin, the *muktuk* (200 to 300 pounds from a large narwhal) is eaten locally. The surplus is sold to settlements further south. Long ago, it was the ideal leather for dog team traces. It remained supple in very cold weather and did not stretch when wet (for these reasons one of the first commercial uses of narwhal leather early in this century was for ski bindings). Oil rendered from narwhal blubber was the Inuit's finest fuel. It burnt in their *kudliks*, the large, crescent-shaped stone oil lamps, with an intensely hot, pure white flame.

And long ago, as now, *ivalu*, "narwhal sinew," provided the people with the best thread in the North. Taken from the narwhal's back and carefully cleaned and dried, sinew makes the perfect thread for arctic people because it is extremely strong, molds itself to leather and does not tear it. All fur clothing, boots, dog harnesses, and the skin tents used in former times were sewn with *ivalu*. I've probably walked a few thousand miles in the sealskin boots Tatagat of Grise Fiord sewed for me in 1969, yet all the seams are still perfect. In 1971 Aqatanguak and her friends sewed the sealskin kayak cover with even, closely spaced stitches of sinew thread as their ancestors had for at least 2,000 years; however, they used steel needles and then they used needles of ivory or bone. (Canadian Inuit now often use extra-strength, waxed dental floss instead of sinew, but it is not nearly as strong.)

On August 10, the first snowstorm of the season sweeps across the land. The caches at Kangerdluqssuaq are full of meat and fat, provisions for the long, dark winter. In late September ice rims the bay and the whales begin to leave. Although narwhals are whales of the ice, if they linger too long in a bay or inlet, the fall ice can trap and kill them. When ice grows across the entrance to an inlet or bay and cuts the whales off from the sea beyond, or if ice links many islands and forms a contiguous belt so broad that the whales cannot swim beneath it to the open sea, then the whales are trapped in a *savssat*, a term derived from the verb *sapivâ*, which means "to bar his way." "We have seen 1,000 animals trapped this way," wrote Peter Freuchen. "One can hear the

"The whole existence of the Polar Eskimos depends on [the narwhal] . . . they get all their necessaries of life from it."

— CHRISTIAN VIBE, Danish scientist, 1940

A little girl helps her mother lash a new kayak cover onto the wooden frame.

noise the unfortunate animals make for miles."

Narwhals can breathe beneath newly formed ice. Using their melons, the resilient, fat-cushioned bulge on the forehead, they bend the ice upward, creating air-filled cupolas and domes. Using their melons as battering rams, narwhals can break ice six to seven inches thick. But as the cold increases, the ice becomes too thick to smash, the whales' pools of open water diminish daily in size, and the frantic animals struggle desperately to reach the life-giving air.

In 1943, a savssat was discovered in Vaigat, the strait north of Disko Island on Greenland's west coast. The newspaper *Grønlandsposten* reported that the crowded whales "emerged so close to each other that some of them would be lifted on the backs of the others and turned a somersault . . . It seethed, blobbed and splashed in the opening." Although narwhals are the main victims, other whales, too, are caught in savssats. In 1750, noted the Danish historian Finn Gad, a large savssat "saved the Egedesminde population from the usual famine." More than 1,000 belugas were taken and 23 bowhead whales; the natives ate the meat and ". . . the blubber and baleen went to the Dutch."

To find a savssat, said Peter Freuchen, "is the dream of any Eskimo." It meant easy hunting, marvelous feasts and ample stores that banished the specter of famine for a year or more. Freuchen and his companions found a savssat in Melville Bay in 1911. "The sea was boiling with the frantic animals fighting for air," he wrote. The whales showed no fear "and the bloodbath lasted for four days and nights." On the west coast of Greenland, recalled the Danish scientist Morton P. Porsild, "The winter of 1914–1915 was so extraordinary that even old people do not remember its like." Two large savssats formed and men hunted day and night. "One young hunter killed on one day five large males and took merely the tusks . . . His profit for that day's work amounted to

Tens of thousands of dovekies sit upon snow slopes in northern Greenland. When frightened, they rush down the mountain slopes like an avian avalanche.

A few dovekie colonies in the Far North number millions of birds. The chubby little seabirds are an important food for northwest Greenland's Polar Inuit, the northernmost people on earth.

five months' wages for a day laborer in Greenland." Altogether, said Porsild, ". . . over 1,000 animals were killed at the two savssats."

In the vastness of the North most savssats, of course, remain undetected. The whales struggle to keep their breathing hole open. If it freezes shut, they suffocate. But ice may shift, a crack can form and along it the whales may escape to open water. On rare occasions another enemy hunts narwhals at a savssat. During the winter of 1920–21, reported the trader Henry Toke Munn, the Pond Inlet Inuit were short of food and were "relieved . . . by the discovery of twenty-one young narwhal hauled out on the ice by a [polar] bear, which was shot. He had evidently taken them out one by one as they came up for air . . . Each one of these young narwhal weighed several hundred pounds. . . ."

The last savssat in the Thule region was in Inglefield Bay in the 1920s when my old friend Masautsiaq was only a boy. He traveled to the savssat with his father Ootah, who had been with Robert Peary to the North Pole, which the marvelously realistic Polar Inuit call Kingmersoriartorfigssuak, "the place where one only eats dogs." The trapped whales were mostly *tugalik*, "tusked males," and the men hunted for weeks in the deep-blue dusk of the arctic night. A half-century had passed, but Masautsiaq recalled the endless feasts with the nostalgic glow of one who might remember a 20-course banquet at the Ritz. "We ate so much we were quite sick," he said, "and our stomachs were always large and swollen and we were very very happy." There had been another year, he once told me, when whaling failed, when the caches were empty, when the only food in camp was a few chunks of ancient, amber-brown blubber. The little boy had lived for weeks on arctic hare dung dipped into rancid oil "and I cried at night with hunger and I did not want to die."

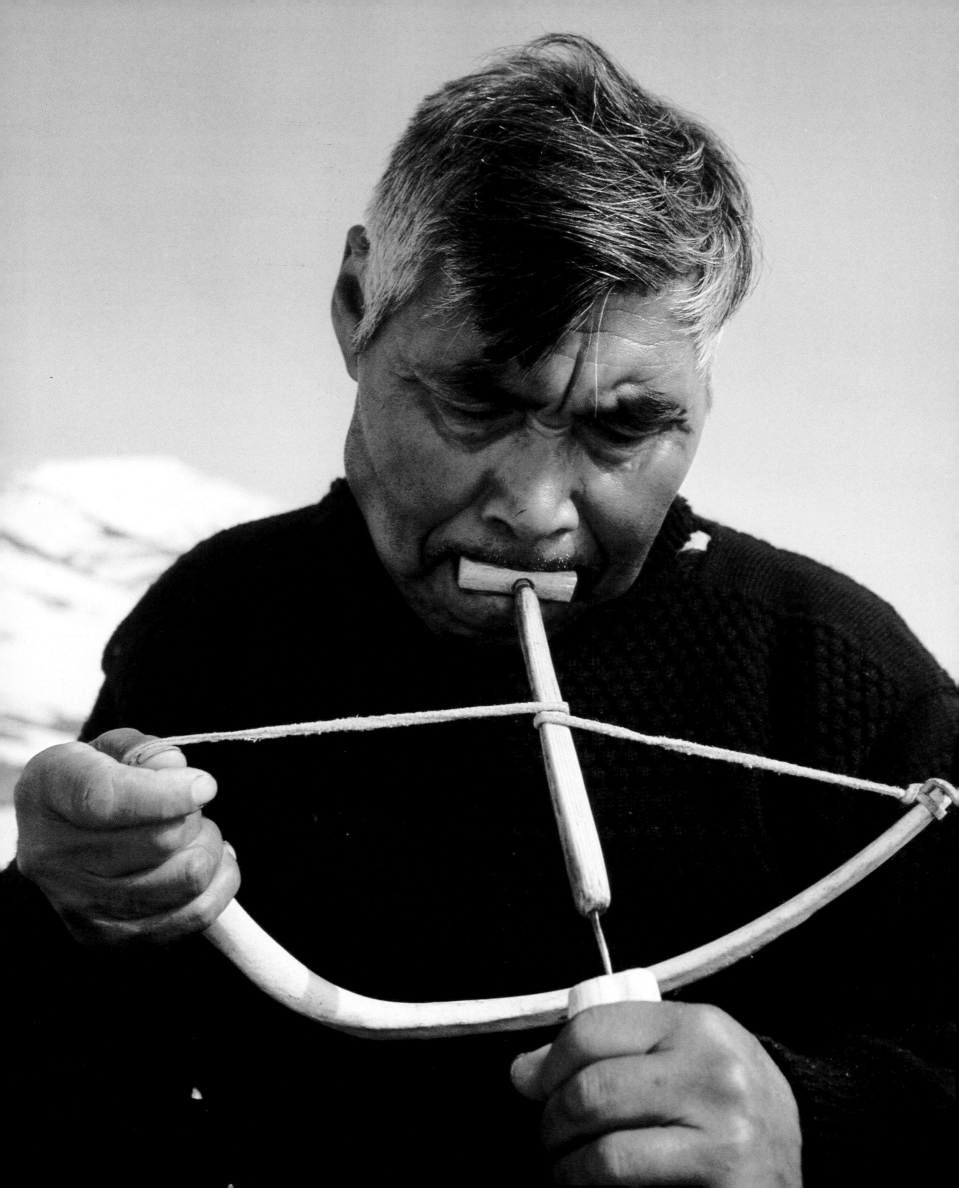

Above: *The narwhal's tusk is cleaned and polished. Once sold as unicorn horn, the spiraled ivory tusk is still eagerly bought by collectors.*

Opposite: *Using a traditional bowdrill, a Polar Inuk makes an ivory harpoon.*

THE VIKING CONNECTION

They came out of the North in sleek dragon ships, wild fearless marauders who pillaged and burned, and all Europe prayed, "*A furore Normannorum libera nos, Domine*"—"From the fury of the Northmen deliver us, O Lord!" They traveled far. The mighty *rus*, the Viking rowers, founded the Kievan state and gave their name to Russia. They were master traders. Each year they met their Arab counterparts from Baghdad and Damascus, from Cairo and Samarkand, on the upper Volga. The Arab merchant-diplomat Ibn-Fadlan saw them in 822 and wrote, "I have never seen more perfect physical specimens, tall as date palms and blond and ruddy."

The Norsemen brought goods of great value: slaves and honey, furs and amber, polar bear skins, live gyrfalcons from Norway and Iceland, walrus ivory and, occasionally, the infinitely precious "unicorn horns" that were really narwhal tusks from Greenland. The Arabs knew the genuine article. The true unicorn horn, said the 13th-century Arab geographer al-Qazwini, is "sharp at the point and thicker at the bottom, with raised striae outside and a hollow within."

The rationale for the Norsemen's great journeys is best summarized in that 13th-century Icelandic compendium of lore and wisdom, *The King's Mirror*, where a father tells his son, "If you wish to know what men seek in that land [Greenland], why men journey thither in so great peril of their lives, it is the threefold nature of man that draws him . . . One part thereof is the spirit of rivalry and the desire for fame . . . Another part is the desire for knowledge . . . The third part is the desire for gain; for men seek after riches in every place where they learn that profit is to be had, even though there is great danger in it."

It was this desire for knowledge, gain and fame that prompted a Norseman named Floki in about 862 to seek land in the unknown northern seas. He sailed northwest from the then already known Faroe Islands and, after a few days, using a mariner's stratagem as old as Noah, released a caged raven. The bird flew back to the Faroes. Floki sailed on and released a second raven, which circled a long time and then returned to the ship. A third raven set free a few days later rose high into the sky and flew off to the northwest. Floki, henceforth known as "Raven-Floki," followed the bird and discovered and named Iceland.

Above: Like a wave-carved Viking dragon ship, an iceberg rides the sea off Baffin Island.

Opposite: The Thule Culture Inuit were superb sea mammal hunters. Age-bleached bowhead vertebrae speak of long-ago meals.

Iceland was quickly explored and settled by the land-hungry Norsemen. A trickle of narwhal tusks began to leave the island and reached continental Europe quietly in the infinitely more precious and saleable guise of "unicorn horns." These augmented the meager supplies that came from arctic Russia and from the Siberian coast. Some tusks were found on beaches, the imperishable remains of dead narwhals washed ashore over eons of time. Other tusks, said the French author Isaac de la Peyrère, who lived in Copenhagen in the mid-17th century and who wrote extensively about Iceland and Greenland, "were brought by the floating ice from Greenland to Iceland." Perhaps these were tusks of narwhals that had died in savssats.

Among the latecomers to Iceland were Thorvald and his teenage son Erik, known as "the Red" because he had red hair and a fiery temper. Both left home hurriedly "because of some killings," as a saga reports. Erik was soon involved in another feud and was banished for three years from Iceland. Following reports of land to the west, he discovered Greenland, sailed south around Cape Farewell and traveled up west Greenland's deeply indented coast.

After giving it the enticing name "Greenland," Erik returned to it in 986 with 14 ships and 400 settlers, their cattle and their chattels. They settled in two regions, the Eastern Settlement in the present Julianehåb district and, further north, the Western Settlement in the Godthåb (now Nuuk) region. Both were in the relatively mild southwesternmost part of Greenland. The colonists were subsistence farmers and hunters. In about 1100, when the colony was at its peak, it had 300 farms, 16 churches, a cathedral at Gardar, the bishop's seat, a nunnery, a monastery, and altogether about 3,000 people who, in this remote outpost that lacked wood, metal and soil suitable for agriculture, tried to lead a modified version of contemporary north European life. "But," notes the unknown author of *The King's Mirror*, "in Greenland . . . everything that comes from other lands is dear there; for the country lies so distant from other lands that men seldom visit it."

The Greenlanders imported wood, grain, iron, clothes, malt, wine, church vestments and such trinkets and adornments as they could afford. They exported fox furs, sealskins and seal oil, dried fish, butter, cheese, and a heavy woollen cloth called *wadmal*, all goods of low value that could not begin to match the value of imports. The real treasures of their land and sea, coveted and paid for in gold and bars of silver by European nobles and Arab princes, were live polar bears and polar bear skins, walrus tusks and walrus hides (the best material for ship's cables), live gyrfalcons and, most precious and rare, narwhal tusks.

To obtain these costly vital goods, the Vikings rowed and sailed far north to Nordrsetur, a region shrouded in secrecy and mystery, for while the Vikings were usually volubly boastful about their travels and exploits, they were mute about their trips to Nordrsetur. The reason for this was, no doubt, the secrecy

Formerly narwhal "tusks were looked upon to be the horns of the fabulous Land-unicorn . . . and sold excessive dear to the gentry . . ."

— DAVID CRANTZ, Moravian missionary to Greenland, 1768

"All the landowners in Greenland had great ships built for voyages to Nordrsetur," the Far North hunting grounds.

— BJØRN JONSSON, Icelandic writer, 1574–1656

surrounding the trade in narwhal tusks. It was, as the British author Odell Shepard has pointed out, "a business in which it did not pay to advertise." It would have been disastrous had the truth leaked out that the marvelous unicorn horns were, in fact, merely the teeth of an arctic whale.

That trips to Nordrsetur were frequent and dangerous we can infer from the existence of a man named Lodinn, popularly known as Lika-Lodinn, "Corpse-Lodinn." His business was to search, for a fee, the northern beaches, collect the bodies of drowned sailors and bring them to south Greenland for burial in consecrated ground. The Icelandic writer Bjørn Jonsson (1574–1656) in his *Annals of Greenland*, based on old sources, wrote, "All the landowners in Greenland had great ships built for voyages to Nordrsetur . . . furnished with all manner of hunting gear . . ." It is recorded that in 1266 the Norse hunters ventured even further north than usual, traveled through dense fog and when they finally sighted land, it was a shore with "many glaciers and seals and white bears." They returned with a valuable cargo of live polar bears, sealskins and walrus ivory. The church authorities at Gardar were so impressed with this rich haul, they promptly sent out a major expedition of their own that probably went far into Melville Bay. The travelers saw many walruses, bowhead whales and seals, but there were "so many [polar] bears that they dared not venture ashore."

Finn Gad, the Danish historian and author of the immensely detailed, four-volume *The History of Greenland*, states flatly that from the "northbound hunting expeditions . . . large quantities of walrus and narwhal ivory were usually brought back by the hunters." The walrus ivory is well documented. Greenland paid its tithes to the papal see in walrus ivory and contributed to at least two crusades to the Holy Land with donations of walrus ivory. It was also the colony's second most important export. Walrus ivory, dense-grained, beautiful and ever-lasting, was widely used to carve chess sets and madonnas, crosier handles for Christian bishops and sword handles for Muslim princes.

But neither narwhals nor narwhal tusks, probably Greenland's most valuable export, are ever mentioned in the sagas or reports. We would not know that such a trade existed if it were not for a few facts, some tantalizing hints and some reasonable conjectures. As of about the year 1000, unicorn horns were widely available in Europe and Arabia. They probably came from Greenland. At about the same time, most unicorns depicted in art carry what is unmistakably the spiraled narwhal tusk. In an addendum to his *Gesta Hamburgensis*, the history of his see that reached far into the north, Bishop Adam of Bremen said in 1070 that Viking hunters went to the far north of Greenland "in order to kill white bears and tanwallen," by which he probably meant *tandhvalen*, toothed whales or narwhals. And we know that two *knorrir*, the large (50- to 60-foot) Norse trading ships, carrying cargoes of "unicorn horns" from Greenland were wrecked upon Iceland's coast.

Someone at the narwhal hunters' camp in northwest Greenland is always looking for whales.

Bones of narwhals, walruses, seals and bowhead whales lie upon the floor of an ancient Thule Culture house on Knud Peninsula, Ellesmere Island.

The Canadian archeologist Peter Schledermann found Viking artifacts in some of these 900-year-old Thule Culture houses on Skraeling Island.

The Icelandic Annals for the year 1242 state that a ship with a cargo of "unicorn horns" was wrecked near Iceland in a storm and that some of the horns were recovered. The second report, in the *Specimen Islandiae Historicum* by Arngrimr Jonsson, published in Amsterdam in 1643 but based on very old sources, is much more detailed because Arnhald, first bishop of Iceland, was aboard the ship that was smashed in 1126 against Iceland's rugged coast. The bishop survived but many sailors drowned, and their bodies and part of the cargo were washed up in a marsh, afterwards known as the Pool of Corpses. Among the items salvaged were many narwhal tusks (*dentes balenarum*) that were "very precious." All were "inscribed in runic letters with an indelible red gum so that each sailor might know his own at the end of the voyage."

To keep a major trade secret intact for 500 years, and to sell during all that time narwhal tusks from Greenland as unicorn horns from China, was no mean feat. As a result of all this secrecy, Nordrsetur remains a region wrapped in mystery. No record tells how far north the Vikings went or whether they hunted narwhals or obtained the precious tusks in trade from Inuit. But we know a little and can guess a lot. In 1824 the Inuk Pelimut discovered a small stone with a runic inscription in a cairn upon the island of Kingigtorssuaq near Upernavik, 700 miles north of the Western Settlement. The short inscription tells of three Norse hunters who built the cairn in April (of about 1300) and who must have spent the winter there; ice would have made it impossible to travel so far north by boat so early in the season.

The Vikings had met Inuit and did not like them. They called them Skraelings, a contemptuous term that meant "a dwarfish, troll-like people." The Inuit "were swarthy, evil-looking men with wiry hair. They had large eyes and broad cheeks." (What the Inuit had to say about the tall, blond, bearded Vikings we unfortunately do not know. Ibn Fadlan, the fastidious Arab, considered them "the filthiest of God's creatures.")

The Norsemen were, no doubt, perfectly able to catch and kill polar bears and the walruses that sleep so soundly on drifting floes and are easily approached. Whether they had the time and the skill to successfully hunt the shy, fast-swimming narwhals, is much more doubtful. The experienced, highly trained British and American whalers of the 19th century rarely lowered their boats for narwhals; they knew from experience that these swift, easily spooked whales usually eluded them. Instead, they bought tusks from the Inuit who were expert narwhal hunters. The natives ate the whales, the white men got the tusks. In 1903, the Canadian explorer A.P. Low observed that in addition to receiving in trade large numbers of narwhal tusks from Canadian Inuit (as many as 400 tusks in a single year), "the Baffin bay whalers obtain a considerable number of narwhal horns from the natives of north Greenland, the best place being in the vicinity of Cape York . . ." in northernmost Melville Bay.

For their trips to Nordrsetur, the Norse used sailing ships or six-oared boats,

"Greenland has always been very productive in horn, which they call unicorn-horn."

— ISAAC DE LA PEYRÈRE, French author, 1647

both much too slow and noisy for consistently successful narwhal hunting. Also, to reach the narwhals' summering grounds in northernmost Baffin Bay and probably Kane Basin between Ellesmere Island and Greenland, the Norsemen had to sail and row 1,200 miles or more from their Western Settlement in the Godthåb region. It would have left them little time for narwhal hunting. It is therefore a reasonable assumption that they obtained many or most of the narwhal tusks in trade from the Inuit, who prized nothing higher in the world than wood and metal, and thanks to their trade with Europe, the Greenland colonists had both.

In the summer of 1978, the Canadian archaeologist Peter Schledermann worked with meticulous care upon the remains of an Inuit house of the Thule Culture period on tiny Skraeling Island in Alexandra Fiord. This site on the east coast of central Ellesmere Island in Canada's High Arctic, less than 800 miles from the North Pole, is "one of the most interesting archaeological sites in North America" and an area "with the northernmost major prehistoric settlements so far discovered." Suddenly his trowel struck metal, two slightly rusted, interlocking rings and, said Schledermann, "in more than 15 years of archaeological exploration I can recall no greater prize . . . The rings had obviously come from a suit of chain mail, the typical armor of medieval Europe."

Subsequent seasons on Skraeling Island and at the equally important prehistoric sites on the nearby Knud Peninsula close to a game-rich polynya, yielded many Norse artifacts: boat rivets, knife blades, a woodworker's plane from about 1200, and a piece of woollen cloth radiocarbon dated at about 1250 "and

Cutting up white whales after a successful hunt. A print made in 1966 by Paulosie Sivua of Povungnituk on the east coast of Hudson Bay.

*A pod of narwhals surges through the arctic
sea. Vikings probably obtained narwhal tusks
in trade from Inuit. Janet Foster/Masterfile*

At birth the narwhal calf is nearly five feet long and weighs about 180 pounds. Animals Animals © Doug Allan

of a type of weave common to the Viking colony in southwest Greenland." Since then other Norse objects have been found in the remains of ancient Inuit houses in Canada's highest Arctic, including a pair of bronze scales which the British archaeologist David Wilson has said were "part of the standard equipment of any [Viking] trader."

I visited Skraeling Island in the summer of 1989 and climbed a hill overlooking the ancient house ruins. They were surrounded by the bleached bones of bowhead whales, of walruses and narwhals, remains of long-ago meals. The entrance passages of many of the stone, bone and sod houses were still clearly visible. Here, until the bitter weather of the Little Ice Age drove them to Greenland, had lived the ancestors of the Polar Inuit, the most skillful narwhal hunters of the North.

Earlier in 1989 my wife and I had been in Central Asia and other parts of the former Soviet Union retracing the ancient trade routes that brought walrus and narwhal tusks from the arctic coasts of Russia and Siberia to the markets of Central Asia, China, the Middle East and western Europe. In Samarkand in Central Asia, once capital of Tamarlane's great empire, several ancient trade routes had crossed. Along the famous Silk Road came goods from China. Another route led from Samarkand along the Syr Darya River and across vast steppes to Bulgar on the upper Volga where Arab and Viking traders met and exchanged slaves, furs, falcons, amber and sometimes "unicorn horns" for gold and silver, for artfully crafted bronze pots, and for those colorful rings, brooches, baubles, bangles and beads the Norsemen loved so much. The Vikings, one 10th-century Arab observed, "will go to any length to get hold of colored beads."

It was mid-August when I was on Skraeling Island, a gloomy, silent night, the light soft bluish-gray. Moist snow fell gently upon the ancient Thule houses. Walruses, squabbling on packed floes, bellowed in the distance. Suddenly I heard the distinctive, explosive "pooff," "pooff," "pooff" of breathing narwhals; 16 whales in two pods swam past the island towards the food-rich polynya near Knud Peninsula.

Schledermann believes the Norsemen may have reached Skraeling Island about 900 years ago and traded there with Inuit. In one Thule Culture ruin he found "a small carved wooden head" dated from around 1100. "Although plainly Inuit in style," wrote Schledermann, "the face to me seems strongly Nordic. It is as if the carver had seen a Norseman with his own eyes and sought to capture that startling vision forever in wood."

I believe that if the Norsemen did come to Skraeling Island and other similarly remote Thule settlements, they came primarily for narwhal tusks. Nothing else was sufficiently valuable to make such long and risky trips attractive. Perhaps some of the "unicorn horns" I had seen in the treasuries of Europe, mounted in gold and sparkling with diamonds and other precious stones, had

"The Baffin bay whalers obtain a considerable number of narwhal horns from the natives of north Greenland . . ."

— A.P. Low, Canadian geologist and explorer, 1903

Warmly dressed in pants of polar bear skin, a reindeer parka, sealskin boots and mitts, a Polar Inuk will spend days at the ice edge, waiting for narwhals to come near.

Alexandra Fiord, Ellesmere Island, where,
centuries ago, Vikings may have obtained
narwhal tusks from Thule Culture Inuit.

Sculpted ice drifts serenely in a fog-shrouded
Baffin Island bay.

been obtained nine centuries ago by Inuit narwhal hunters then living on this remote and lonely island and had been bartered to the Norse for wood and metal.

The most amazing find so far was made on Bathurst Island in Canada's High Arctic. There a team of archaeologists headed by Robert McGhee of the Canadian Museum of Civilization found in an ancient Inuit house a small bronze pot made in Central Asia. Arabs probably brought it to the Volga, Vikings to Greenland, and about 800 or 900 years ago on a trip to Nordrsetur, a Viking trader may have met Inuit and exchanged the little bronze pot for that most precious of all arctic goods, a narwhal tusk.

After 1300, fate dealt harshly with Greenland's Norse colonists. Once the Vikings had been the terror of the seas. Now English and Scots pirates looted Norse ships and plundered Norse settlements in Iceland. The climate became much colder. The Black Death killed a third of Europe's population. Fewer and fewer ships made the long, perilous trip to Greenland. The culturally cold-adapted Inuit prospered, pushed further south and clashed with the settlers. The Icelandic Annals for 1379 record that "the Skraelings attacked the Greenlanders, killed eighteen of them, and carried off two boys." The Western Settlement was abandoned. The lucrative trips to Nordrsetur ceased, and the once-vital people withered away. When in 1492, the year Columbus discovered America, Pope Alexander VI expressed concern for his Greenland flock *in fine mundi*, "at the end of the world," the last had died in lonely despair, ill-nourished and rachitic.

Skraeling Island, near Ellesmere Island, in Canada's High Arctic. Here Vikings and Inuit may have traded 800 or 900 years ago.

THE BEGINNINGS OF DOUBT

Above: *The long ivory tusk of the narwhal male is unique. It is the only straight, spiraled horn in all creation.* Flip Nicklin

Opposite: *A narwhal dives steeply; for an instant its fluke rises high into the air.* Flip Nicklin

Long ago, people believed that there existed a balance between land and sea and that the animals of the land had their counterparts in the sea. The analogues were often strange and many were unknown, but then the world was largely unexplored and people were quite confident that in due time the missing matches would be found. There were land horses and sea horses (an old name for walruses), land cows and sea cows, land bears and sea bears (an old name for fur seals), land lions and sea lions, land serpents and sea serpents, and there were men and maids on land and mermen and mermaids in the sea. It therefore came as no surprise when, to complement the famous land unicorn, a sea unicorn was discovered. It merely confirmed a long-standing theory.

In 1576, the Elizabethan explorer Sir Martin Frobisher set out with two ships to find the Northwest Passage, a northern shortcut to Cathay and the fabulous wealth of the East. He discovered Baffin Island and returned with a large black stone, which one assayer claimed to be rich in gold. Backed by many, including Queen Elizabeth I, Frobisher made two more trips, in 1577 and 1578, the last one with 15 ships and 400 men. They mined 2,000 tons of worthless ore (a mixture of pyroxenite and amphibolite now often called "fool's gold") on a tiny island in Frobisher Bay, to the utter amazement of the local Inuit who call it to this day Kodlunarn, "the white man's island."

On July 22, 1577, "upon another small Islande," Frobisher's men "founde a great deade fishe which had in his nose a horne streight & torquet, of lengthe two yardes lacking two ynches, being broken in the top, where we might perceiue it hollowe, into which some of our Saylers putting spiders, they presently dyed . . . by virtue whereof, we supposed it to be the sea Unicorne." Upon his return to England, Frobisher presented the "unicorn horn" to his queen, who commanded that it be called a "jewel" and placed in her treasury.

Spiders were then believed to be extremely poisonous. During the examination into the famous murder of Sir Thomas Overbury in 1613, one witness testified "that the countess [Frances Howard] wished him to get the strongest poison that he could . . ." and he had given her "seven big spiders." Since unicorn horn "killed" poisons, it was supposed to be lethal to spiders, and the "spider test" was often employed to ensure the genuineness of the horns.

In 1584, half mad with the memory of innumerable murders, haunted by ghosts and fears and omens, Tsar Ivan IV, the Terrible, summoned 60 "witches" from Lapland to foretell his future. They said he would die on March 18. "I am poisoned with disease," the tsar complained, according to the English ambassador Sir Jerome Horsey, and he called for "his staff royal, a unicorn's horn garnished with fair diamonds, rubies, sapphires, emeralds and other precious stones." He ordered his physician to scrape a circle on the table with the horn and to place spiders within the circle. All the spiders died, but the tsar said: "It is too late . . . [the unicorn horn] will not preserve me." He rallied briefly and played chess with his courtiers, but suddenly fell backward in a faint and soon after, reported Horsey, he was "stark dead." It was the evening of March 17.

Spider tests were not always conclusive and could, in fact, be quite embarrassing. When George Villiers, 2nd duke of Buckingham and favorite of King Charles II, was admitted to the prestigious Royal Society on June 5, 1661, he presented the society with a piece of unicorn horn. The scientists scraped some powder from the horn, made a circle with it on the floor and put a spider in the center. It scurried away, unharmed — and so did all the other spiders in subsequent experiments. Only one, it was noted, "made some stay on the powder."

After the Norse colonies in Greenland had flickered out in misery and isolation, there was a brief hiatus and then the flow of narwhal tusks resumed. Dutch and Danish traders began to obtain them from the Greenland Inuit. In 1656, the French author César de Rochefort watched a Dutch ship from Vlissingen, just back from Greenland, being unloaded. From its capacious hold came bundles of sealskins, polar bear pelts, and even an Inuit kayak. "But that which is most rare and precious," wrote de Rochefort, "that is the large quantity of these . . . horns of that fish called the 'sea unicorn.'" Such tusks, said de Rochefort, had been sent to Paris where they were "well received," for not only were they treasured as curiosities, they were also excellent as medicine: "Several doctors and apothecaries of Denmark and Germany who have made extensive tests . . . claim that these horns combat poison and that they have all the properties commonly attributed to the horn of the Land Unicorn."

This was the ultimate irony. Now there were two "unicorn horns" on the market: "land unicorn horns," still worth many times their weight in gold and "sea unicorn horns," an acceptable and cheaper substitute, the panacea of the poor. Both were, of course, the narwhal tusk, but that fact somehow eluded the equally deluded princes and the plebs. Demand and prices for unicorn horns remained high. An electoral prince of Saxony paid 100,000 thalers for his horn, the Republic of Venice in 1597 offered 30,000 ducats for a perfect horn and could not get one at that price, and in 1664 the French import duty on unicorn's horn was 50 sous per pound.

Belief in the power and the glory of the "true unicorn horn" remained

"Upon another small Islande . . . [we] found a great deade fishe . . . [with a] horne wreathed and strayte, like in fashion to a Taper made of waxe, and maye truely be thoughte to be the sea Unicorne."

— CAPTAIN GEORGE BEST, member of Martin Frobisher's expedition to Baffin Island, 1577

"Several doctors and apothecaries in Denmark and Germany who have made extensive tests [of sea unicorn horns] claim . . . that they have all the properties commonly attributed to the horn of the Land Unicorn."

— CESAR DE ROCHEFORT, French author, 1656

unshaken, but some buyers exercised caution for fear of acquiring fraudulent "imitation" horns. The total faith of the Middle Ages yielded to the questing spirit of the Renaissance. James I of England (1566–1625) paid more than £10,000 for his unicorn horn, then a sum that would buy a castle. To assuage some nagging doubts about the genuineness of his horn, the king poisoned a servant and then fed him powder from the unicorn horn. The servant died and the king complained bitterly that he had been cheated. Even in India unicorn horns were no longer bought on faith alone. In 1615 an English whaling ship returned from Spitsbergen with a beautiful narwhal tusk. In 1616 a ship of the British East India Company took the tusk to India and offered it as "unicorn horn" to the ruler Mukarrab Khan for 5,000 rupees. He poisoned a pigeon, a goat and a man, and then gave them unicorn powder as an antidote. All died and he refused to buy the "fraudulent" horn.

In 1619, the year the Danish explorer Jens Munk left on his ill-fated expedition to Hudson Bay (only three of the 65 expedition members survived), narwhal tusks, according to an English account of the expedition, "were much in request among the physicians; and the Danes used . . . to sell them at a very high rate; and be always very cautious of discovering to the world that these horns or teeth belonged to a sea-fish, which is the reason they were taken for the true unicorn." But slowly, insidiously, the odious word spread that even the genuine unicorn horns were, in fact, fish teeth.

The French author Isaac de la Peyrère, who lived for a long time in Denmark, wrote in 1647 that a few years before that date the New Greenland Company in Copenhagen had sent one of its partners to Moscow with a set of narwhal tusks, including one particularly beautiful "horn" valued at 6,000 rix-dollars. The "Grand Duke of Muscovy thought it very fine" but before buying it "had it examined by his physician. He, knowing more about it than the others, told the Grand Duke that it was the tooth of a fish, and the envoy returned to Copenhagen without selling anything." His partners were furious. "You managed badly," they told the luckless salesman. "Why did you not give two or three hundred ducats to the physician, to persuade him that they were from unicorns."

The façade of faith cracked, the truth dribbled out, and the most ancient and best kept of all trade secrets was slowly exposed; the unicorn horn was really the tooth of an arctic whale. To stem this ugly rumor, the Danish merchants appealed to the highly respected scientist and regius professor Ole Wurm for a verdict that, they were confident, would name the narwhal tusk as genuine unicorn horn and restore faith in their precious product. It was a dreadful tactical mistake. Ole Wurm was totally honest, totally incorruptible. He wrote in the 1630s to his "former Pupil" Thorlac Scalonius, bishop of Hole in Iceland, asking for information about the narwhal. The bishop sent a painting of the whale and explained that the Icelanders called it a "narhual."

Overleaf: *Sea and ice glow as the sun sets behind the mountains of Alexandra Fiord on Ellesmere Island, an area rich in sea mammals.*

Wurm borrowed the skull and horn of a "unicorn," valued at 8,000 rix-dollars, from Fris, the high chancellor of Denmark. He examined it with great care and finally, after lengthy studies, told Isaac de la Peyrère that "these animals which bear these horns in Greenland . . . were fish." It was shocking news. "I had great disputes with him," wrote de la Peyrère, "because it overturns the opinions of all the old naturalists who have treated of unicorns . . . and it clashes with several passages of Holy Scripture, which can only be understood as having reference to unicorns with four feet." It was no use. In 1638, Wurm presented his dissertation on "The Horn of the Unicorn" in Copenhagen and exposed it as the tusk of the narwhal.

The unicorn was gravely wounded; the aura created by total faith and clever and sustained deceit that had maintained its legend and the price of its miraculous horn for more than a thousand years was damaged beyond repair. Since the increase of commerce with Greenland and Spitsbergen, wrote another Danish professor, Thomas Bartholin in 1645, "our merchants have filled whole cargo vessels with this alleged horn of recent years and would import it into Europe as genuine unicorn had not experts torn away the mask and recognized the tusk as originating from the ocean." And, Professor Bartholin added with a final, brutal twist, it is "that tusk . . . which is preserved in the treasuries of various rulers." In the pharmacies of Frankfurt, Germany, the price of unicorn horn per half ounce dropped from 64 florins in 1612, to 32 florins in 1643, to 4 florins in 1669. The German lexicographer Zedler in his 1734 *Grosses Universal Lexicon* stated that unicorn horns which were formerly sold for tens of thousands of thalers were then only worth 20 to 25 thalers each. In 1746, "unicorn horn" was, at the suggestion of the English Royal Society of Physicians, quietly dropped from Britain's pharmacopoeia.

With the unicorn defrocked, the famous "horn" became a mere curio, the walking stick of the affluent burgher or the discerning nobleman. The narwhal's "ivory," noted George Brown Goode, assistant director of the United States National Museum in 1880, "is made into canes and other articles of ornament. The supply in this country is chiefly imported from Denmark." In New York in 1880, a good tusk sold for $50.

Even in their new, more modest role, narwhal tusks were magnificent. The British biologist W. Jardin wrote in 1837 that "the ivory of the narwhal is esteemed superior to that of the elephant, and far surpasses it in all its qualities; it possesses extreme density and hardness, has dazzling whiteness, which does not pass into yellow, and easily receives a very high polish." Charles Maurice de Talleyrand-Périgord, prince of Benevento (1754–1838), probably France's greatest diplomat, was severely injured in a childhood accident. He walked with a special boot on his crippled right foot and supported himself with a very precious walking stick, a narwhal tusk with a gold pommel and a steel ferrule. It is preserved to this day at Talleyrand's Château de Valençay.

Thousands of narwhal tusks were stored in this building on northern Baffin Island in the early years of this century. From here about three tons of narwhal ivory were shipped annually to Britain. National Archives of Canada/C 10972

As bowheads became rare and profits dwindled, whalers built shore stations, such as this one at Cape Haven on Baffin Island in 1903, where products of the region, including narwhal tusks were gathered. National Archives of Canada/PA 53586

In 1616 the East India Company took a narwhal tusk from Spitsbergen to India and offered it as "unicorn horn" to Mukarrab Khan. "He tried its effects on a poisoned pigeon, goat, and man, who all died. So he refused to buy it."

— SIR MARTIN CONWAY, English author and explorer, 1906

During Norse time and until the middle of the 19th century most narwhal tusks came from Greenland. After the British explorers John Ross in 1818 and William Edward Parry in 1819 reached the narwhals' summering grounds and opened the way for British and American whalers, most narwhal tusks came from Baffin Island. By the late 19th century, Pond Inlet had become the main center of both the narwhal hunt and the trade in narwhal tusks and hides. The British explorer Sir Leopold M'Clintock, searching for the missing Franklin expedition, stopped at Pond Inlet in 1858 and found that the Inuit there carried on a brisk trade in narwhal tusks with passing whalers. An Inuk called Awahlah "showed us about thirty horns in his tent, and said he had many more at other stations . . . Rod-iron is very valuable to the Esquimaux for spears and lances, and narwhals' horn very tempting to the seamen, not only as valuable curiosities, but the ivory is worth half a crown a pound." The Canadian sea mammal specialists Randall R. Reeves and Edward Mitchell have pointed out that "as part of his contract, one nineteenth-century Scottish whaling captain was guaranteed a 15 percent commission on any narwhal ivory he brought home."

At first this trade was carried on primarily by whalers as a lucrative sideline. They arrived from Scotland in early summer, hunted bowhead whales and, said the Canadian explorer and trader J.E. Bernier in 1910, secured "from the natives bear, wolf, seal, walrus, and narwhal skins and ivory, then coast along southward and return to Scotland in November." By 1912, to the intense annoyance of the monopolistically inclined Hudson's Bay Company, "free traders" muscled in on the trade in narwhal tusks. There were three "opponents"

A narwhal killed by Inuit hunters in 1924 is winched onto the ice. National Archives of Canada/PA 99111

Marble Island was a center of 19th-century
whaling in Hudson Bay. Whalers were buried
on tiny Deadman Island in the bay beyond.

The narwhal's tusk "is the only product of value to civilized man, this being made into canes and other articles of ornament."

— GEORGE BROWN GOODE, assistant director, United States National Museum, 1880

as the "Bay men" called them: Captain Bernier; Henry Toke Munn, a shrewd and experienced trader; and the gloomy, suspicious Robert S. Janes, obsessed with the idea that he would find gold, and who had 292 narwhal tusks in his possession when he was murdered by Inuit in 1920.

In 1912, these three men shipped three tons of ivory from Pond Inlet, the tusks of about 600 narwhals. In 1923, the thoroughly aggrieved Hudson's Bay Company manager in Pond Inlet wrote to his superiors: "The Narwhal industry has been developed . . . almost to its limit. Furs are merely a side issue. Five or six hundred Narwhal would be considered as only an ordinary year's hunt, the Oil, Ivory and Skins of which would be worth approximately $18,000. There is, I understand, a special market in Peterhead [Scotland] for narwhal skins and that they are finally sold in France for making very fine gloves." P.L. Simmonds, in that fount of fascinating information, *Animal Products: Their Preparation, Commercial Uses, and Value*, published in London in 1877, says that narwhal leather compares "favorably with the best French kid in beauty, cheapness and durability, whilst it is in high repute for the strongest shooting-boots."

Most of the narwhal tusks obtained by the free traders on Baffin Island, and by the whalers from Inuit in the Canadian Arctic and in Greenland, were eventually sold to China and Japan, where the belief in unicorns and the potency of their horns both as medicine and to defeat poison continued undiminished. The period from 1900 to 1925 saw the all-time peak of narwhal hunting, partly because during this time large numbers of whales were trapped in savssats in Greenland and Canada and killed by Inuit hunters. When the *Albert*, Henry Toke Munn's boat, arrived in Scotland in 1921, she carried 201 beluga hides and two "Lorry Loads narwhal Ivory." And the British author Odell Shepard said that in 1923 an American ship exploring the coasts of Greenland picked up "scores of tusks. Hundreds of them are to be seen at present in the London docks."

The riled Hudson's Bay Company manager at Pond Inlet told his superiors in 1923 that "this is an industry that we would rather leave for the present and concentrate on furs alone, but as it is the main support of our opponent [Janes had been murdered and Bernier had sold his share of the business to Munn], it is imperative that we interest ourselves in it and endeavor to take as much of it as possible, so as to eventually make it not worth our opponent's while to continue coming to the country." He got his wish the selfsame year. Munn sold his business to the Hudson's Bay Company, and the Bay man at Pond Inlet, heaving, no doubt, a great sigh of relief, went back to doing what all Bay men like doing best — buying furs. The narwhal tusk business dwindled to insignificance. Still, those had been deadly years. According to Mitchell and Reeves ". . . a total of 10,970 narwhals [were] killed in the Baffin Bay-Davis Strait region during the decade 1915–1924. We consider this as a conservative estimate."

A Polar Inuit hunter returns to camp.

*Equipped with guns and whale harpoons,
Polar Inuit go to the floe edge to hunt
narwhals.*

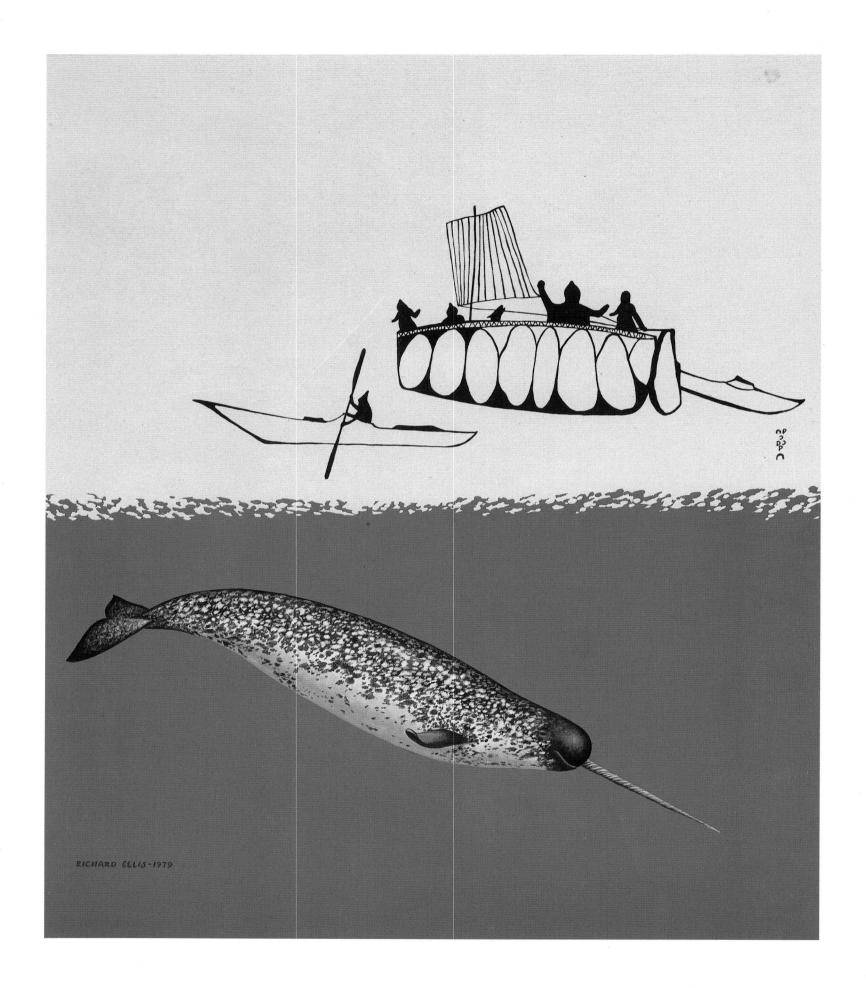

RICHARD ELLIS-1979

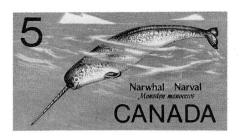

RETURN TO KOLUKTOO

It is the summer of 1988. I have returned to Koluktoo Bay where, nearly a quarter century ago, Brian Beck, David Robb and I captured narwhals in gigantic nets. The data we amassed in the first extensive physiological study of these then little known whales, collated and evaluated by Dr. Arthur Mansfield and published in many scientific papers and reports, are still the basis of most narwhal research. Sometimes in recent scientific studies I see familiar figures of the size-age-weight relationship in narwhals and remember how the three of us struggled weighing whales upon Koluktoo's wind-lashed beach.

Now I am back to capture whales again. We sit on the grassy slope of Bruce Head, the great promontory that juts out into Koluktoo Bay. Far beneath, our great net waits for whales in the dark water of the bay. The ethos of the times has changed. We will not kill the whales, but capture them alive, affix small radio transmitters to their tusks and release them. It is the project, never before attempted, of two of Canada's foremost scientists, Dr. Michael Kingsley of the Department of Fisheries and Oceans and Dr. Malcolm Ramsay of the University of Saskatchewan, assisted by Holly Cleator of Winnipeg's Freshwater Institute, by a summer student, and by the Inuk Sheatie Tagak and other Inuit of Pond Inlet. The great annual migrations of narwhals are already known in general outline, a mosaic of knowledge assembled from hundreds of observations. But the detailed evidence that can only be obtained by knowing the routes taken by marked animals is missing. The North is changing fast; this knowledge may be essential to protect the whales in future when their migration routes and arctic shipping lanes may overlap.

Koluktoo Bay remains unchanged. The weather is still vile; three days after we arrived a storm blew down my tent, a déjà vu I did not need. Today is beautiful—the sky cool blue, wave-sculpted pieces of ice glitter upon the dark water of the bay, the space seems infinite, the air as clean and fresh as chilled champagne. We watch and wait. Great furry bumblebees drone busily from bloom to bloom gathering the last nectar of summer.

I sat upon this grassy slope in 1965 and watched the whales swim past the point of Bruce Head, the polished tusk tips of the males glinting in the water. Since then I have pursued the unicorn and its legend to the far corners of the earth. I asked for unicorn horn in a dark and dingy "drug" store in Bombay,

India, and with a knowing smile a grizzled man produced a small bamboo box that contained a grayish powder. It was rhinoceros horn, and he assured me it would do wonders for my libido. "It will make you strong, sir!" he said.

I have seen the results of this belief in Africa where poachers, now equipped with submachine guns, have reduced the population of black rhinoceroses by 95 percent in 15 years, to satisfy the demand for the "all healing unicorn horn" in the East. One rhino horn was worth $20,000 in 1988 in a region of Africa where the average annual income was $300 a year. I had been to the Ujung Kulon Nature Reserve on Java where poorly paid but dedicated wardens sometimes risk their lives to protect the last 65 Javan rhinoceroses from the poachers. I had visited the treasuries of Europe and had seen the narwhal tusks, often set in gold and covered with jewels, that, as "unicorn horns," had safeguarded princes from poison. And throughout my travels I had marveled at the power and persistence of old legends and beliefs.

The radio crackles. Sheatie Tagak adjusts it and speaks with Pond Inlet Inuit who live at a summer narwhal hunting camp to the north of us. "Whales are coming to Koluktoo Bay," Sheatie informs us. "Many have passed the other camp." He turns to me and smiles. "Today we catch *tugalik*!" he says.

Pond Inlet, the Inuit settlement, has changed beyond belief in the years since I last visited. It is a large modern village now. Cars and trucks rumble down its streets, a taxi takes people to the airport. There is a fine hotel and large stores amply stocked with expensive southern foods brought regularly by cargo planes. Most Inuit work for the many government departments, some for the lead-zinc mine at Nanisivik, west of Pond Inlet. A polar bear skin drying on a porch is one of the few reminders that this is still a village of arctic hunters. Most men hunt part-time, on weekends, during holidays, on time taken off from other work. They travel far and fast; the slow sled dogs and kayaks have been replaced by expensive high-powered motorboats and snowmobiles.

Each spring groups of tourists come to Pond Inlet to watch narwhals. Inuit outfitters pack the visitors carefully in large open plywood boxes, lined with sleeping bags and foam rubber mattresses, load them onto long *komatiks*, the traditional Inuit sleds, and haul them by snowmobile to the floe edge, the limit of landfast ice. Round, whiskered heads surface in the sea; young ringed seals, the easily killed 'silver-jars' of commerce, stare in large-eyed wonder at the humans. A bearded seal cruises along the ice edge, rolls forward and dives. Pure white ivory gulls fly by with shrill ternlike cries. Long rows of murres, neatly spaced like pearls upon a string, fly busily across the water. In the distance, narwhals swim in the polynya. The tourists focus spotting scopes and long lenses. They are ecstatic. They have seen the fabled narwhal, the "sea unicorn." The ancient magic still works.

In New York one day, as an experiment, I looked for unicorns. In one leisurely afternoon, strolling through Manhattan, I counted 17: a plush unicorn in a toy

"As men . . . we must tell our children not to waste meat in the hunt . . ."

— APPAQ, Pond Inlet Inuk, talking to biologist Kerry Finley, 1979

"Among the different kinds of whales some reckon the unicorn . . . It is a pretty large fish . . . and yields good fat . . ."

— THOMAS PENNANT, author of *Arctic Zoology*, published in London in 1784

store; a unicorn at the entrance to a bar; unicorns in store windows, on calendars and books; tiny silver unicorns upon a Burgundy-red tie in the window of a very expensive clothing store; a large poster, prominently displayed, shows a white, shining unicorn, its flashing, spiraled horn radiating power. At a party in New York the black writer Dudley Randall is told by a critic to write about timeless themes and symbols, such as the "white unicorn," and shoots back "why not about black unicorns?" The poet Anne Morrow Lindbergh writes about "The Unicorn in Captivity." A lovely, fragile unicorn and all its symbolism are central to Tennessee Williams's play *The Glass Menagerie*.

After the tourists leave, the Pond Inlet Inuit hunt the narwhals as they swim in leads among the ice. Canada's Narwhal Protection Regulations, established in 1976, allot to all settlements where narwhals were traditionally hunted a quota: altogether, Canadian Inuit may take 542 narwhals each year. Pond Inlet and Arctic Bay on northern Baffin Island have always been the major centers of the narwhal hunt; the hunters from these two settlements may take 100 whales each. Many hunters, especially the young ones, shoot at long range, at 325 feet or more. They kill or wound a lot of whales (which are not counted in the quota) and only retrieve a few. One study shows that 42 percent of all narwhals in the Pond Inlet region are bullet scarred. The people do not keep the meat. Unlike their Greenland cousins, most Canadian Inuit do not like the taste of narwhal meat, and now that they do not have sled dogs, the meat — a thousand pounds or more per whale — is dumped into the sea.

The narwhals are killed to get the *muktuk*, the delicious, vitamin-rich skin and, above all, the spiraled tusks of the males. At present, say the sea mammal specialists Randall R. Reeves and Edward Mitchell in a recent article, the narwhal hunt in Canada "is primarily a trophy hunt." In Pond Inlet the price for tusks soared from $2 per pound in 1960 (a very large tusk weighs about 20 pounds) to $400 per pound in 1982. In 1983, the European Economic Community banned the import of all marine ivory, and the price for narwhal tusks in Pond Inlet slipped to $80 per pound. (In August 1989, on my return from Skraeling Island, I noticed a 5½-foot-long, beautifully polished narwhal tusk for sale in the souvenir shop at the airport in Resolute on Cornwallis Island. The price was $1,900.)

The hunt may be wasteful, but it does not menace the survival of the narwhals. Tom Strong, a biologist with Canada's Department of Fisheries and Oceans, has made extensive narwhal surveys. The narwhal population counts during the past 20 years give about the same results, indicating that the population, despite the hunt, is stable. To the Inuit the hunt is vital, not, perhaps, economically anymore, but culturally. It is their link to land and sea, their last link to the past, it is what makes them *Inuit*, "the people," the hunters of the North. Take away the hunt and the Inuit as Inuit will probably cease to be. "Of course I hunt narwhals," Sheatie Tagak says. "Hunting is my life."

Pond Inlet, Baffin Island, the Canadian center of the narwhal hunt, is a thoroughly modern settlement with dish antennae and large stores.

The cross in St. Jude's Anglican Cathedral in Iqaluit, Baffin Island, is made of narwhal tusks. The altar railings are two polished dog team sleds.

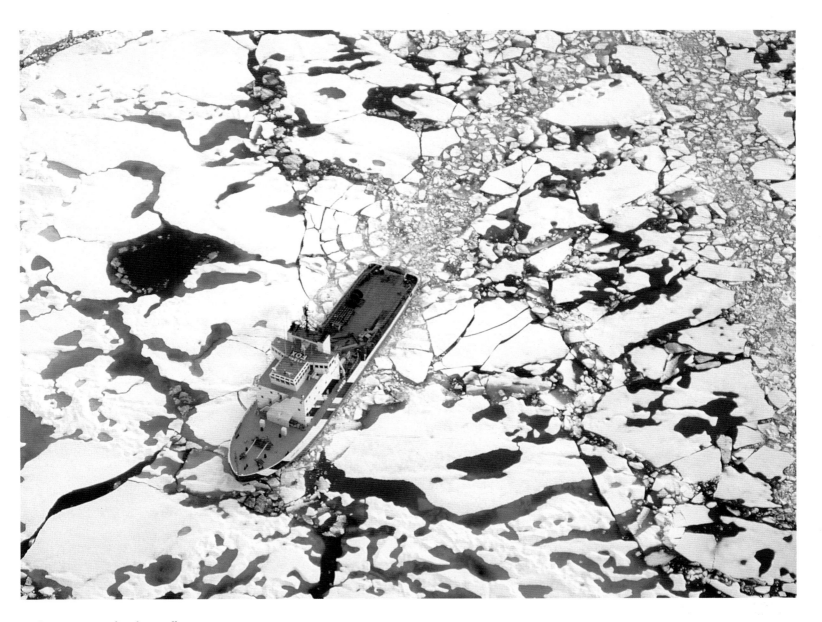

In future, giant icebreakers will carve year-round shipping lanes into the arctic ice for convoys of ships carrying liquefied natural gas. These artificial leads may change narwhal migrations.

The magnificent white gyrfalcon was one of the greatest treasures of the North. Vikings captured them in Iceland and Greenland for sale to European and Arab princes.

Dr. Michael Kingsley affixes a small radio transmitter to the narwhal's tusk to study the animal's as yet poorly known migrations. The transmitter is designed to drop off after a few months.

Although the hunt may not threaten the narwhals' survival, there are other threats, peculiar to our age. Pollution of the seas is now worldwide. Studies in the Baltic Sea have shown that increasing concentrations of polychlorinated biphenols (PCBs) "have significantly reduced the reproductive rates in ringed seals." Professor G. Pirelli of Bern in Switzerland writes in a recent paper that "The zinc mine at Nanisivik [west of Pond Inlet] alone pours every year 35,000 tons of poisonous substances into the sea" — in an area that is a major summering and perhaps calving ground of narwhals.

Vast quantities of natural gas have been discovered in the Arctic. By the year 2000 it is expected that great fleets of L.N.G. (liquefied natural gas) tankers will ply Lancaster Sound, the famous Northwest Passage and the region Parry rightly called "the headquarters of the whales." About 19,000 of the world's estimated 25,000 to 30,000 narwhals pass through it on their spring and fall migrations. The great fleets of tankers will be led, perhaps summer and winter, by as many as 30 Class 10 icebreakers, 150,000 horsepower vessels capable of

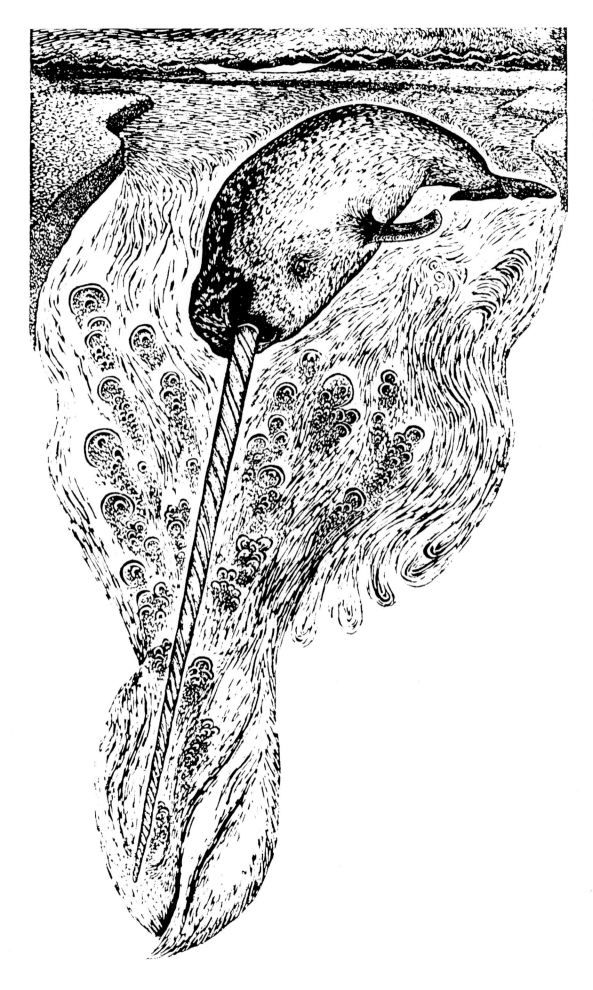

A wood engraving by the Canadian artist Michiel Oudemans, who has spent weeks in the Arctic observing narwhals.

"Our merchants have filled whole cargo vessels with [narwhal tusks] . . . and would import it into Europe as genuine unicorn, had not experts torn away the mask . . ."

— THOMAS BARTHOLIN, Danish scientist, 1645

plowing through ice ten feet thick, creating artificial leads and lanes that narwhals may be tempted to follow, possibly to death.

"Every whale everywhere moves in a sea of total sound," wrote the American biologist Victor B. Scheffer. "From the moment of its birth until its final hour, day and night, it hears the endless orchestra of life around its massive frame . . ." Now shrill and alien sounds will mingle with this orchestra of life. The scientist B. Møhl in his study, "Marine Mammals and Noise," believes that the L.N.G. tankers' motor noises may block communications between the gregarious narwhals and other marine animals "more than 100 m apart." He further suggests that the noise level may result in temporary or possibly permanent hearing damage and in nausea induced by infra-sound.

Sheatie calls. A single narwhal swims close to shore directly towards our net. Abruptly, the long row of styrofoam floats is yanked beneath the surface. The whale is caught. We race to the shore and launch the two boats. The team hauls up the great net and the struggling whale. They pin the animal between the boats to immobilize its powerful, slamming tail. The head is raised, dark and shiny, covered with mesh. The whale breathes in explosive gusts through its crescent-shaped blowhole. Michael Kingsley clamps a small, tubular, stainless steel-encased radio transmitter to the narwhal's four-foot tusk. The net is cut and with one immensely powerful push of its heart-shaped flukes, the whale dives down into the sea.

It is the first time a narwhal has been equipped for radio telemetry. "Today you helped to make biological history!" an exultant Malcolm Ramsay tells the summer student. For three days the scientists follow the movements of the whale by helicopter. Then the signal becomes weak and finally it ceases. Perhaps the transmitter slipped from the smooth tusk. Perhaps the fast-swimming whale bent or broke the small fiberglass-protected antenna. There will be other years. Other narwhals will be equipped with radio transmitters and their movements tracked, not by helicopter but by satellite. The sea unicorn's every movement will be monitored from space.

We return to Pond Inlet. I have supper at Akpaleeapik's house. In 1967 he and his brother Akeeagok took me along on the last great polar bear hunt made by Canadian Inuit; now such hunts are history, part of a vanished way of life. Today Akpaleeapik lives in a large, comfortable three-bedroom house, similar to suburban houses in the south. We drink tea and talk about "the old days" when we lived in snowhouses and tents, when we lived by the hunt alone and often ate raw blubber and raw meat. The talk turns to narwhals: the narwhal we have caught and released and the narwhals hunted during the summer by the Pond Inlet Inuit. A Japanese dealer has visited the settlements recently, Akpaleeapik tells me. He bought not only entire tusks, valued as curios, but broken tusks and pieces of narwhal tusks. "He told us," the old Inuk hunter says, "that in Japan they make a wonderful medicine from these horns."

BIBLIOGRAPHY

Aristotle. *The Works of Aristotle.* 2 vols. Chicago: Encyclopaedia Brittanica, 1952.

Beer, Rüdiger Robert. *Unicorn: Myth And Reality.* New York: Van Nostrand Reinhold Company, 1977.

Bernier, J.E. *Reports on the Dominion Government Expedition to Arctic Islands and the Hudson Strait on Board C.G.S. 'ARCTIC' 1906–1907.* Ottawa: King's Printer, 1909.

Biggar, H.P. *The Voyages of the Cabots and of the Corte-Reals to North America and Greenland 1497–1503.* Paris: Macon, Protat Frères, 1903.

Boas, Franz. *The Central Eskimo.* Sixth Annual Report of the Bureau of Ethnology, Smithsonian Institution. 1888. Reprint. Lincoln: University of Nebraska Press, 1964.

Bonner, J.T. "The Horn Of The Unicorn." *Scientific American.* 184 (1951): 42-43.

Borges, Jorge Luis. *The Book Of Imaginary Beings.* New York: E.P. Dutton & Co., 1969.

Born, E.W. "Narwhal." *Whalewatcher; Journal of the American Cetacean Society.* 21 (Spring 1987).

Brower, Kenneth, and Curtsinger, Bill. *Wake of the Whale.* New York: Friends of the Earth, 1979.

Bruemmer, Fred. *Encounters with Arctic Animals.* Toronto: McGraw-Hill Ryerson, 1972.

———. *Arctic Animals.* Toronto: McClelland and Stewart, 1986.

———. *World of the Polar Bear.* Toronto: Key Porter Books, 1989.

Chappell, Edward. *Narrative of a Voyage to Hudson's Bay in His Majesty's Ship Rosamund.* London: J. Mawman, 1817.

Charlevoix, François Xavier de. *Journal of a Voyage to North America.* 2 vols. Chicago: The Caxton Club, 1923.

Churchill, A. *An Account of a Most Dangerous Voyage Performed by the Famous Captain John Monck in the Years 1619 and 1620.* A Collection of Voyages and Travels, vol. I. Printed by Assignment. London, 1732.

Collings, D.W. "Historic Narwhal Tusks." Trans. Suffolk Nat. Soc. 1933. 2:52-54.

Conway, Martin. *No Man's Land.* Cambridge: Cambridge University Press, 1906.

Crantz, David. *The History Of Greenland.* 2 vols. London: Brethren's Society, 1768.

Davis, Rolph A.; Finlay, Kerwin J.; and Richardson, W. John. "The Present Status and Future Management of Arctic Marine Mammals." Prepared for the Science Advisory Board of the Northwest Territories, Yellowknife, N.W.T. Report No. 3, January 1980.

Dunbabin, Thomas. "Canada's Horn of the Unicorn." *The Beaver,* Spring 1956.

Durant, Mary. *In Pursuit of the Mous, the Snaile, and the Clamm.* New York: Meredith Press, 1968.

———. "Scouting for an Elixir." *Audubon Magazine,* January 1983.

Egede, Hans. *A Description of Greenland.* London: T. and J. Allman, 1818.

Ellis, Richard. *The Book of Whales.* New York: Alfred A. Knopf, 1980.

Emboden, William A. *Bizarre Plants.* New York: Macmillan Publishing Co., 1974.

Ettinghausen, Richard. *The Unicorn.* Studies in Muslim Iconography, vol. 1. Washington: Smithsonian Institution, 1950.

Farb, Peter. *The Land, Wildlife, and Peoples of the Bible.* New York: Harper & Row, 1967.

Finley, Kerwin J., and Renaud, Wayne E., "Marine Mammals Inhabiting the Bay North Water in Winter." *Arctic,* December 1980.

Finley, Kerwin J.; Davis, Rolph A.; and Silverman, Helen B. *Aspects of the Narwhal Hunt in the Eastern Canadian Arctic.* International Whaling Commission report 30, 1980: 459-64.

Finley, Kerwin J., and Miller, Gary W. *The 1979 Hunt for Narwhals (Monodon monoceros) and an Examination of Harpoon Gun Technology Near Pond Inlet, Northern Baffin Island.* International Whaling Commission report 32, 1982.

Ford, John, and Ford, Deborah. "Narwhal: Unicorn of the Arctic Seas." *National Geographic Magazine,* March 1986.

Foxe, Luke. *North-Vvest Foxe.* 1635. Reprint. London: S.R. Publishers Ltd., Johnson Reprint Corporation, 1965.

Fraser, F.C. *British Whales, Dolphins & Porpoises.* London: British Museum (Natural History), 1976.

Freeman, Margaret B. *The Unicorn Tapestries.* New York: The Metropolitan Museum of Art, 1976.

Freuchen, Peter. *Ice Floes and Flaming Water.* New York: Julian Messner, 1954.

Freuchen, Peter, and Salomonson, Finn. *The Arctic Year.* New York: G.P. Putnam's Sons, 1958.

Gad, Finn. *The History Of Greenland.* 2 vols. Montreal: McGill-Queen's University Press, 1971.

Greendale, R.G., and Brousseau-Greendale, C. *Observations of Marine Mammals at Cape Hay, Bylot Island During the Summer of 1976.* Fisheries and Marine Service technical report 680.

Hakluyt, Richard. *Voyages.* 8 vols. London: J.M. Dent & Sons Ltd., 1962.

Haley, Delphine, ed. *Marine Mammals of Eastern North Pacific and Arctic Waters.* Seattle: Pacific Search Press, 1986.

Hansen, Thorkild. *The Way To Hudson Bay.* New York: Harcourt, Brace & World, 1970.

Hathaway, Nancy. *The Unicorn.* Middlesex, England: Penguin Books, 1982.

Hearne, Samuel. *A Journey from Prince of Wales's Fort in Hudson's Bay to the Northern Ocean 1769, 1770, 1771, 1772.* 1795. Reprint. Toronto: Macmillan Company of Canada, 1958.

Herbert, Wally. *Across the Top of the World.* London: Longmans Group, 1969.

Ingstad, Helge. *Land under the Pole Star.* New York: St. Martin's Press, 1966.

Jones, Gwyn. *The Norse Atlantic Saga.* Oxford: Oxford University Press, 1986.

Kingsley, Michael C.S., and Ramsay, Malcolm. "The Spiral in the Tusk of the Narwhal." *Arctic,* September 1988.

Konungs Skuggsja (The King's Mirror). Translated by Laurence M. Larson. New York: American-Scandinavian Foundation, 1917.

Laing, John. *An Account of a Voyage to Spitzbergen.* London: J. Mawman, 1815.

Lamont, James. *Seasons with the Sea-Horses.* London: Hurst and Blacklett, 1861.

Laufer, Berthold. *Arabic and Chinese Trade in Walrus and Narwhal Ivory.* Vol. XIV. London: E.J. Brill, 1913.

Lewinson, Richard. *Animals, Men And Myths.* New York: Harper & Brothers, 1954.

Ley, Willy. *Dawn of Zoology.* Englewood Cliffs, N.J.: Prentice-Hall, 1968.

——— . *Exotic Zoology.* New York: The Viking Press, 1962.

——— . *The Lungfish, the Dodo, and the Unicorn.* New York: The Viking Press, 1948.

Lopez, Barry. *Arctic Dreams.* New York: Charles Scribner's Sons, 1986.

Low, A.P. *Cruise of the Neptune.* Ottawa: Government Printing Bureau, 1906.

Lyall, Ernie. *An Arctic Man.* Edmonton: Hurtig Publishers, 1979.

Lyon, G.F. *The Private Journal of Captain G.F. Lyon of H.M.S. Hecla During the Recent Voyage of Discovery Under Captain Parry.* London: John Murray, 1824.

MacCulloch, John A., ed. *The Mythology of All Races.* 13 vols. Boston: Marshall Jones Company, 1932.

M'Clintock, Leopold F. *The Voyage of the "Fox" in the Arctic Seas in Search of Franklin and His Companions.* London: John Murray, 1875.

Mansfield, A.W.; Smith, T.G.; and Beck, Brian. "The Narwhal, Monodon monoceros, in Eastern Canadian Waters." *Journal of the Fisheries Research Board of Canada* (1975), pp. 1041-46.

Markham, Clements R. *The Voyages of William Baffin.* London: Hakluyt Society, 1881.

Martens, Friedrich. *Journal d'un Voyage au Spitzbergen et au Groenlandt.* 1671. Reprint. Amsterdam: Jean Frederic Bernard, 1725.

Martin, Esmond B. "They're Killing Off The Rhino." *National Geographic Magazine,* March 1984.

Massie, Suzanne. *Land of the Firebird.* New York: Simon and Schuster, 1982.

Melville, Herman. *Moby Dick.* London: Collins, 1953.

Meyer, Charles R. *Whaling and the Art of Scrimshaw.* New York: Henry Z. Walk, 1976.

Mitchell, Edward; and Reeves, Randall R. *Catch History and Cumulative Catch Estimates of Initial Population Size of Cetaceans in the Eastern Canadian Arctic.* International Whaling Commission report 31, 1981: 645-82.

Munn, Henry Toke. *Prairie Trails and Arctic By-Ways.* London: Hurst and Blackett, 1932.

Nansen, Fridtjof. *Farthest North.* 2 vols. New York: Harper & Brothers, 1897.

——— . *In Northern Mists.* London: William Heinemann, 1911.

Neruda, Pablo. *Memoirs.* Harmondsworth, Middlesex: Penguin Books, 1978.

Nishiwaki, M. "Tusks Of Unicorn (Monodon monoceros) owned by Prince Takamatsu." *Jour. Mam. Soc. Japan.* 4 (1969), pp. 159-62.

Nordenskiöld, A.E. *The Voyage of the Vega Round Asia and Europe.* London: Macmillan & Co., 1883.

Parry, William Edward. *A Journal of a Voyage for the Discovery of a North-West Passage from the Atlantic to the Pacific, 1819–1820.* London: John Murray, 1821.

Pedersen, Alwin. *Polar Animals.* New York: Taplinger Publishing Co., Inc., 1966.

Pennant, Thomas. *Arctic Zoology.* London: Henry Hughs, 1784.

Perry, Richard. *The World of the Walrus.* London: Cassel & Company, 1967.

Peyrère, Isaac de la. "Description Of Greenland." 1647. In *A Collection of Documents on Spitzbergen and Greenland,* edited by Adam White. London: The Hakluyt Society, 1855.

Pilleri, G. "Auf Baffinland Zur Erforschung Des Narwals (Monodon monoceros)." Ostermundingen, Berne: Verlag des Hirnanatomischen Institutes, 1983.

Porsild, Morton P. "On Savssats: A Crowding of Arctic Animals at Holes in the Sea Ice." *The Geographical Review,* September 1918.

——— . "Scattered Observations on Narwhals." *Journal of Mammalogy* 3 (1922): 8-13.

Power, Eileen. *Medieval People.* New York: Barnes & Noble, 1965.

Raven, H.C. "Northward for Narwhal." *Natural History Magazine,* Jan./Feb. 1927.

Reeves, Randall R. "The Narwhal; The Strangest Cetacean." In *Wildlife '77*. The Danbury Press, 1977.

———. "Narwhal." In "Alaska Whales and Whaling." *Alaska Geographic* 5.

Reeves, Randall R., and Tracey, Sharon. "Mammalian Species." No. 127. pp. 1-7. American Society of Mammalogists, 1980.

Reeves, Randall R., and Mitchell, Edward. "The Whale Behind the Tusk." *Natural History*, August 1981.

———. "Cetaceans of Canada." Communications Directorate. Department of Fisheries & Oceans. DFO-512. UW 5. Ottawa, 1987.

Rochefort, César de. *Histoire Naturelle Et Morale Des Iles Antilles*. Rotterdam, 1665.

Ross, John. *A Voyage of Discovery . . . for the Purpose of Exploring Baffin's Bay . . .* London: Longman, Hurst, Rees, Orme and Brown, 1819.

Ross, W. Gillies. *Arctic Whalers Icy Seas*. Toronto: Irwin Publishing, 1985.

Rugoff, Milton, ed. *The Travels of Marco Polo*. New York: The New American Library of World Literature, 1961.

Sanderson, Ivan T. *Follow the Whale*. Boston: Little, Brown and Company, 1956.

Scammon, Charles M. *The Marine Mammals of the Northwestern Coast of North America*. 1874. Reprint. New York: Dover Publications, 1968.

Scherman, Katharine. *Spring on an Arctic Island*. Boston: Little, Brown and Company, 1956.

Schledermann, Peter. "Eskimo and Viking Finds in the High Arctic." *National Geographic*, May 1981.

Scoresby, William, Jr. *An Account of the Arctic Regions*. Edinburgh: Archibald Constable and Company, 1820.

———. *Journal of a Voyage to the Northern Whale-Fishery*. Edinburgh: Archibald Constable and Co., 1823.

Sergeant, D.E., and Williams, G.A. "Two Recent Ice Entrapments of Narwhals, Monodon monoceros, in Arctic Canada." *Canadian Field-Naturalist* 97(4): 459-60.

Sergeant, D.E., and Hay, K. "Migratory Sea Mammal Populations in Lancaster Sound." ESCOM Report No. A1-21. Indian & Northern Affairs. Ottawa, 1979.

Shepard, Odell. *The Lore of the Unicorn*. 1930. Reprint. New York: Harper & Row, 1979.

Shepherd, Anthony. *A Flight of Unicorns*. London: Elek Books, 1965.

Silis, Ivars. "Narwhal Hunters of Greenland." *National Geographic Magazine*, April 1984.

Silverberg, Robert. *The Auk, the Dodo, and the Oryx*. New York: Thomas Y. Crowell Company, 1967.

Silverman, H.B., and Dunbar, M.J. "Aggressive Tusk Use by the Narwhal (Monodon monoceros L.). *Nature*, March 1980.

Simmonds, P.L. *Animal Products. Their Preparation, Commercial Uses, and Value*. London: Chapman and Hall, 1877.

Smith, Charles Edward. *From the Deep of the Sea*. Edinburgh: Paul Harris Publishing, 1977.

Soper, J. Dewey. "A Faunal Investigation of Southern Baffin Island." National Museum of Canada. Bulletin No. 53. Ottawa, 1928.

Stefansson, Vilhjalmur. *The Three Voyages of Martin Frobisher*. London: The Argonaut Press, 1938.

Steltner, Hermann, et al. "Killer Whales, Orcinus orca, Prey on Narwhals, Monodon monoceros: An Eyewitness Account." *Canadian Field-Naturalist* 98: 458-62.

Stirling, Ian, and Calvert, Wendy. "Environmental Threats to Marine Mammals in the Canadian Arctic." *Polar Record* 21: 433-49.

Stirling, Ian, and Cleator, Holly, eds. *Polynyas in the Canadian Arctic*. Environment Canada. Canadian Wildlife Service. Occasional Paper Number 45. Ottawa, 1981.

Strong, John Thomas. "Status of the Narwhal, Monodon monoc-eros, in Canada." *Canadian Field-Naturalist* 102: 391-98.

Sutcliffe, Antony J. *On the track of Ice Age Mammals*. Cambridge, Mass.: Harvard University Press, 1985.

Thompson, C.J.S. *Poison Mysteries in History, Romance and Crime*. Philadelphia: J.B. Lippincott Company, 1924.

———. *The Mystery and Art of the Apothecary*. London: John Lane The Bodley Head, 1929.

Time-Life Books, Editors of. *Magical Beasts*. Alexandria, Virginia: Time-Life Books, 1985.

Tomilin, A.G. *Mammals of the U.S.S.R. and Adjacent Countries*. Jerusalem: Israel Program for Scientific Translations, 1967.

Tremblay, Alfred. *Cruise of the Minnie Maud*. Quebec: The Arctic Exchange and Publishing Ltd., 1921.

Uhlig, Helmut. *Die Seidenstrasse*. Bergisch Gladbach: Gustav Lübbe Verlag, 1986.

Verne, Jules. *20,000 Leagues Under the Sea*. New York: Bantam Books, 1962.

Vibe, Christian, "The Marine Mammals and the Marine Fauna in the Thule District (Northwest Greenland) with Observations on Ice Conditions in 1939-41." Middelelser Om Grønland. Bd. 150. Nr. 6. C.A. Reitzels Forlag. Copenhagen, 1950.

Vietmeyer, Noel D. "Rare Narwhals Inspired Myth of the Unicorn." *Smithsonian*, February 1980.

Walsh, William S. *A Handy Book of Curious Information*. Detroit: Gale Research Co., 1970.

Wernick, Robert, and the Editors of Time-Life Books. *The Vikings*. Alexandria, Virginia: Time-Life Books, 1979.

White, T.H. *The Book of Beasts*. London: Jonathan Cape, 1954.

Wilkinson, Doug. *Land of the Long Day*. New York: Henry Holt and Company, 1956.

Wilson, David. *The Vikings and Their Origins*. London: Thames and Hudson, 1972.

INDEX

Numbers in italics refer to illustrations and photographs.

Other Books By Fred Bruemmer

The Long Hunt
Seasons of the Eskimo
Encounters with Arctic Animals
The Arctic
The Life of the Harp Seal
Children of the North
Summer at Bear River
The Arctic World
Arctic Animals
Seasons of the Seal
World of the Polar Bear